How To Be Captivating

The Ultimate Guide to
Being Irresistible

How To Be Captivating

The Ultimate Guide to Being Irresistible

Shay Allie

SASSY BOOKS

Winchester, UK
Washington, USA

First published by Sassy Books, 2013
Sassy Books is an imprint of John Hunt Publishing Ltd., Laurel House, Station Approach,
Alresford, Hants, SO24 9JH, UK
office1@jhpbooks.net
www.johnhuntpublishing.com
www.sassy-books.com

For distributor details and how to order please visit the 'Ordering' section on our website.

ISBN: 978 1 78099 739 1

A CIP catalogue record for this book is available from the British Library.

Design: Stuart Davies
Illustrations: Marcelo Gorenman
Cover: Biba Hunjan

Printed in the USA by Edwards Brothers Malloy

We operate a distinctive and ethical publishing philosophy in all
areas of our business, from our global network of authors to
production and worldwide distribution.

CONTENTS

This book is dedicated to:

The late Saquina Sacoor-Ahmad – my beloved Nan

Nan was the most beautiful, vivacious, powerful, loving, inspirational, strong and all round incredible woman that I have had the privilege to know. I'd be thrilled to grow up to become half the woman that she was. She was extremely special and all round extraordinary. I will always miss her incredibly.

Introduction

"When a baby is born, it's crying, yet everyone around it is smiling. Live so that you die smiling and leave everyone around you crying."
Saquina Sacoor Ahmad

Nan was one of the most captivating presences I have ever had the privilege to know. At the end of her life, she was the oldest surviving member of the relatively well-known Sacoor family. Her journey through life started though in Jangamo, Mozambique which sadly faced great unrest in the 1970s. On attempting to flee the country, Nan had a devastating accident. The car rolled down a cliff top, left in a complete wreck. She had to have stitches to her head and was paralysed from neck to toe. She was rescued from the wreckage, but was classified as paraplegic and was told that she would never walk again. Instead of a spine, she had screws and metal holding her together.

Nan decided that she didn't like her prognosis. She also decided that she was meant to walk and that she was meant to live life to the full. She asked the physiotherapists to teach her how to walk. They refused, but eventually watched in disbelief as she took her first few steps.

She moved to London a mere two years later. She had an appointment at a leading London hospital. On meeting the doctor, he was convinced he had the wrong patient notes. Nan had arrived at hospital, on public transport, without so much as a walking stick to help her. He was speechless.

Nan died when she decided it was her time to go, over 40 years later. Her funeral was attended by many who were crying. Despite the tears, she had a smile on her face as she was laid to rest. She had indeed touched many with her gifts of wisdom, strength, coupled with her glamour and vivacity.

I always like to tell people that I take after Nan. Unlike her, I'm happy to say that I grew up in London with no civil unrest *or* car accidents. I dreamed, like most little children, of what I wanted to be when I grew up. To some kids that usually meant being a princess, a popstar or a footballer. To me, it meant being a barrister; a woman with the gift of the gab and the ability to defend the needy. It never occurred to me that the career was near impossible to get into, and one where, even if you've qualified, you stand a less than 20% chance of permanent work in the industry. It also never occurred to me that being young, feminine, attractive, and an ethnic mish-mash, didn't exactly fit the mold of a typical barrister. Anything but success was *not* an option, and I would naturally delete from my mind the opinions of others who would tell me otherwise. And you know what? Landing my first job, with what remains one of the top ranked barristers' chambers in the UK, came almost effortlessly. How? I jokingly tell people that I relied on my charm and good looks, which always raises a smile, but there is more truth in that statement than you'd first expect. Now, I want to share with everyone the *real* success formula. Whether you wish for health, your ideal career or the lover of your dreams, you need one key ingredient: a captivating presence.

Someone with a captivating presence turns heads the moment they walk into a room. They know *exactly* how to draw and keep someone's attention. In short, a captivating presence makes you absolutely magnetic. Do you think that sort of magnetism is reserved for only the Oprah's or the Marilyn Monroe's of this world? The good news is that ANYONE can have a captivating presence, no matter what your weight, job, passions, age or musical taste. Throughout this book, you'll learn how to switch ON your own personal brand of magnetism within you, so that the YOU people meet is the one that you really want them to see, the one that is *completely* captivating.

Throughout this book, we are going to work together to make

sure that you can: instantly boost your personal presence so that no matter what room you walk into, not only do you absolutely shine, but you consistently keep everyone captivated. You owe it to yourself, and the world, to die smiling with the world around you crying for the loss of you.

PART 1

BEING CAPTIVATING: THE MINDSET

"Our deepest fear is not that we are inadequate. Our deepest fear is that we are powerful beyond measure. It is our light, not our darkness, that most frightens us. We ask ourselves, who am I to be brilliant, gorgeous, talented and fabulous? Actually, who are you not to be? you're a child of God. Your playing small doesn't serve the world. There's nothing enlightened about shrinking so that other people won't feel insecure around you. We are all meant to shine, as children do. We are born to make manifest the glory of God that is within us. It's not just in some of us; it's in everyone. And as we let our own light shine, we unconsciously give other people permission to do the same. As we are liberated from our own fear, our presence automatically liberates others."

Marianne Williamson, quoted in Nelson Mandela's inaugural speech in 1994.

Chapter 1

"Why am I a failure?"
A Captivating Mindset

"Low self-esteem is like driving through life with your hand-break on."
Maxwell Maltz

Now, for those of you reading this book because your dream is to win the lottery on Friday, your biggest question is probably *'why am I not winning?'* not, *'how could I use mindset work to change up my chances in life?'* Mindset work may not be as thrilling as hitting the lottery jackpot, but it is absolutely fundamental if you want to win the jackpot of life and if you're in the right mindset, I guarantee that you'll enjoy the ride a lot more, whether your numbers come up or not! So, you're at the pub with your friends. You've had a few large glasses of your favourite wine. Are you guilty of saying any, if not all, of the following?

> *"With my luck..." (insert semi-tragic story here)*
> *"It's Sod's law isn't it?"*
> *"Thank God it's Friday – can't wait to get out of the office!"*
> *"I'm a complete failure. I hate everything about my life."*

It's funny how we can suddenly turn into really quite melancholy philosophers with minimal encouragement, isn't it? Seriously though, the reason we've all been there is that one of the biggest human fears that *everyone* faces, is that we're simply not good enough. Some fear they're not good enough to achieve anything positive in life. Some even go as far as creating beliefs and excuses as to *why* they're not good enough. Thankfully, there is a three-step process in order to help you eliminate these beliefs for good and help you to feel fantastic as a result. And of course, feeling fantastic is fundamental to guaranteeing ultimate success in every area of your life.

Step 1: Ask Yourself the Right Questions

We are all the very lucky and privileged owners of the most powerful, intelligent and advanced computers on the planet – our brains. If you ask your brain a question, it will reliably give you the answer to anything that you ask it. It may not always be the right answer, but your internal resources are infinite and you'll always get an answer. How familiar does this conversation sound?

> You: *'Why am I a failure?'*
> Your Brain: *'Because you never get anything right and you're just an idiot.'*
> You: *'That's a bit harsh – are you sure?'*
> Your Brain: *'Yes. You really need to stop trying – you'll just fail again anyway!'*

If this is you, why are you letting that voice in your head, verbally beat you up? So many of us do it, mainly because our brain is an absolute genius at coming up with excuses for why you can't have what you want in life.

So, how would it be if you could change the questions that you ask yourself, and re-frame them in a more positive way? The secret of successful people is to consistently ask *quality* questions.

"Quality questions create a quality life. Successful people ask better questions, and as a result, they get better answers."
Tony Robbins

Once you get the question right, your brain will be forced to come up with quality options, and sometimes even the perfect answer.

Here are some examples of quality questions that you can ask yourself, just to get you started. You'll probably notice that you can come up with many more of your own:

- What are my achievements?
- What are my gifts? How can I share them with the world?
- What am I most grateful for?
- What would my ideal job look like?
- What are the qualities that I would like in my ideal partner?
- How can I get more energy?
- How can I be more healthy and enjoy it?
- Who do I most admire, are there any qualities that they have that I could copy?
- What was I doing when I last felt good about myself? How can I do that more?
- What would I like people to notice about me? How can I ensure that they do notice?

Step 2: Spring-Clean Your Beliefs

I can already hear you saying *'but I like my beliefs thank you very much, Shay!'* Well, if your beliefs are positive, then that's fair enough and you can move onto the next exercise. But what about the little stories and excuses that you tell yourself about your limitations? Sometimes, they are so ingrained in our subconscious, that we think they are real, actual facts. They become our reality because we're so utterly convinced that they're true.

If you are full of stories and excuses as to why you can't do certain things, chances are that you have quite a few unhelpful beliefs. Helpful beliefs can make us reach for the stars, but unhelpful, or limiting beliefs, keep us stuck in a rut.

Laura's Story

Laura believed that life was tough and that bad things always happened to her. She has been blessed with looks that 90% of the population would envy, together with a level of academic intelligence to ensure that she could do well in life if she wanted to. However, her negative views on life mean that she forever attracts the wrong friendships, relationships and working environments. She entered her 30s having had a number of violent relationships and little by way of family and friendship ties, as she had fallen out with the vast majority of them. It was only when she decided to modify her views that her fortunes started to change and I am pleased to say that she has not had any subsequent violent relationships and is now beginning to get her career back on track. Those views were very deeply engrained, although the changes may seem small to some, they are a far cry from the mental place that she was in.

Each belief that you hold only exists because your mind has found some evidence of its truth. The more evidence you have for each of your beliefs, the more you're likely to hold onto them, regardless of whether they are positive or negative.

So, let's get practical. What are your negative beliefs? Be

completely honest with yourself and write down all those things that you say to yourself about why you haven't got the results you want in life. If you can't remember what you say, ask one of the friends you confide in – they're likely to give you a whole list!

Some common negative beliefs include:

- I'm far too shy to do *that*. Only people like [insert name of confident person] would ever do that, and that could never be me.
- Nothing ever works out for me. I don't know what all this law of attraction rubbish is all about because whatever I try, nothing goes my way and that is just life. I have to accept it.
- I don't have the money/time/skills.
- I'm a terrible salesperson. If only I *could* sell, my business would be a storming success, but it's the recession, and people just don't want to buy my stuff.
- No one ever notices me. I think it's because I'm too fat/ugly/boring.

It's important that you're completely honest with yourself. Sometimes the truth isn't pretty, but if you really want to banish this mindset forever, you must acknowledge where you're at first. Once you've done this, for each of your beliefs, ask yourself the following questions:

- What is my belief?
- Is it a belief that's helpful to me?
- What evidence do I have to uphold that belief?
- Is that evidence credible?
- Am I telling myself the real truth by holding this belief?
- If you feel you're telling yourself the real truth, on whose authority is it the real truth?

- Do I want to change my belief?

Once you've taken some time to answer these questions in relation to all your negative beliefs, consider the very last question again; *'Do I want to change my belief?'* Hopefully, you'll answer *'yes'* and be open to replacing your old, crappy belief, with a new empowering one. If the answer is *'no'*, try and think about why this is. Sometimes, it is easier to stay where we are, no matter how bad, than to venture out into the unknown. We are wired to keep ourselves safe, and sometimes that may well involve not taking the risk of trying a new belief. In that sense, try and think about any benefits that this belief is actually bringing you? Sometimes the hardest thing to do is to step out of our comfort zone, but in order to truly reach great heights of success in our lives, this is *exactly* what we have to do.

If you're not afraid to step out of your comfort zone, and you feel that there are no other benefits, then the next question to ask yourself is, why are you so committed to holding onto the negative belief? Are there any alternative beliefs that won't be as damaging?

If you still don't want to change your belief, try imagining what your life will be like in 5, 10 or 20 years if you keep holding onto it. You can use the following questions to fuel your imagination. When answering each question, get creative and think of the *worst* possible thing that could happen if you *do* hold on...

- What will I look like?
- Where will I live?
- What kind of person will I be?
- Is my belief enriching the older me?
- Does my belief stop me from getting what I want?
- Is the belief preventing me from finding happiness?
- Are you avoiding doing things or meeting people because you believe this?
- When you think about your belief in this way, do you really think it's worth holding onto? How much it will cost you?

Now for the fun part. When you have your list of beliefs you want to change, think of a new, empowering belief that you can replace each negative one with.

Remember to:

Support this new belief with as much evidence as you can to verify its truth. Ask your brain for as much evidence as you can find. At the very least, come up with at least 3 more stories to support your new belief, rather than your old one.

Ask for evidence as to why your old belief isn't true. Again, you can simply ask yourself why your old belief isn't true, and your mind will come up with the answers for you. Ask your mind the question with a clear and open heart, to come up with some genuine answers. Some of the techniques in sections 11 and 12 will help clear your mind, if your immediate reaction to this question is *but it is true!*

For additional support, if you're really struggling, you can always ask your friends, family or mentors to help you or work through the exercises within step 3 for additional inspiration.

Ama's Story

Ama was afraid. She believed that if she went for what she wanted, all the people in the world would take advantage of her and that she'd never get anywhere.

Through doing this exercise, she found that if she carried this belief with her, she would always be stuck with a job that she hated, live in a house that she wasn't happy in.

She wanted to change. She decided that a better belief to have would be that God/the universe was supporting her in whatever she wished to do. She backed up this belief by remembering how her parents used to encourage her when she was little, and their faith in her was far more important than the more insignificant people around her, expressing opinions that didn't really mean very much.

One year on, Ama bought a new home and re-arranged her work so that the job, and its timetable, suited her needs.

Don't forget to make your new belief stronger each day by collecting evidence, no matter how small; to make sure your new belief becomes ingrained as fact. Little successes could be as simple as a compliment from your boss, getting that bargain in the sale or even just finding the perfect parking space, just when you need it most! The more evidence you get for your new empowering belief, the stronger it will become. Once you really believe your new belief, you'll start to notice that you're acting and thinking differently, and success becomes effortless!

Step 3: Be Fabulously Happy and Adore Yourself

Do you ever wish you had the voice of Aretha Franklin, the looks of Marilyn Monroe and the brains of Albert Einstein? Well tough, you don't. The good news is, that being you is a fabulous thing. There is no one else in this world that is gifted enough to be you. In the words of Oscar Wilde, *'Be You. Everyone else is taken.'* Being the *real* you, and, therefore, completely unique, is one of the most important aspects of learning to be captivating and attracting the attention that you want. There's no one else in this world that is going to adore you, if you don't start by adoring yourself. So it is essential that you are your own biggest fan. If you think this sounds selfish, think again. If you can't convince yourself that you're a wonderful human being, and great fun to be around, how are you going to convince the world?

If adoring yourself is something that you've always found hard, pour your heart and soul into at least two, if not all of the following exercises, and start telling yourself that you're absolutely worth loving!

Positive Interpretation

Imagine the following situation. A wife is waiting at home for her husband. He is running slightly late. She has two options as to how she interprets his lateness:

Positive: he's probably just held up in traffic and I can't wait to see him!

Negative: I bet he's having an affair with his secretary that *&^%$

If you were the hubby, which version would you rather come home to? If she isn't careful, her thoughts could become a self-fulfilling prophecy. In this example, if hubby came home to a loving wife each night, he is likely to look forward to coming home to her, and if he *were* having an affair, he'd be likely to end it swiftly. On the other hand, if he always comes home to a negative wife, who questions his every move, there may well be an affair with his secretary on the horizon.

The moral of this story is to control your thoughts, and make sure that the meaning you place on the events in your life is positive. This will guarantee that you experience more positive results. Remember, being in a good mood is a choice. Use step one to help you; the quality of the questions that you ask yourself can determine how positive your thoughts are going to be. Life is all about *our* interpretation of things. The only meaning that exists is the meaning that we place on things and events. Try and make them as beautiful as possible.

Daydreaming

One of the most powerful ways to feel good, is to imagine yourself in a place where you're most happy. Take a moment to close your eyes, and visualise yourself in this place. The place could be your local park, beach, or anywhere where you feel relaxed. Close your eyes and take a few deep breaths. Imagine that you're in that place right now. Imagine the colours around you. Imagine the warmth of the sun against your skin. Imagine the sounds that you hear around you. Get lost in your imagination and breathe in the feeling of peacefulness. Try visualising this scene for at least two minutes.

While you're in this state, how do you feel? Chances are that if you're doing this exercise properly, you will be feeling a lot more relaxed than when you started the exercise. Once you have internalised this memory, hold on to the vision and go back to this place any time that you're feeling down.

You can also try visualising your favourite holiday, a time in your life when you were very happy, or simply the type of person you would like to, and are going to be.

Once you have a favourite visualisation, try and start your day by visualising this place, or vision each morning, paying close attention to how it makes you feel. This will ensure that you start every day as you mean to go on – in a warm and positive mood. It's difficult to be sad when you're thinking about such lovely things!

Mirror, Mirror on the Wall

Do you remember the story of *Snow White*? In particular, do you remember her evil stepmother? Every morning she used to look in the mirror and say to herself *'mirror mirror on the wall, who is the fairest of them all?* ' Although she was an evil character, this type of behaviour isn't immediately crazy. You have to admit, she was powerful, wasn't she? You too can have this power, in a positive way of course, by looking into your own mirror. Look deeply into your own eyes, and speak from your heart about what is positive about you. The eyes are said to be the windows of your soul, and this could be one of the most powerful exercises that you do with yourself. No one needs to know that you're doing this, if this feels a little uncomfortable to you. There is no better person to love you than you, so you should be able to look yourself in your own eyes and tell yourself that. It's better to let your words flow from your intuition and your heart rather than reading out anything pre-prepared (you'll be looking into your eyes after all!), but when you're having this conversation, don't forget to mention:

- How great you are
- What a great job you're doing
- How you're so great at coping with everything
- How beautiful you are
- How everyone loves and appreciates everything that you do
- How privileged you are to be you
- Reassure yourself

Creative Writing

If you prefer to write than speak out loud, a great way to boost your mood is to write a creative feel-good piece to yourself. This could be in the form of a letter, telling yourself how great you are, or a letter filled with your wishes for how you want things to be.

You could also ask your closest friends or family, or anyone who thinks highly of you, to write some words about you. You could even share the fact that you're doing this exercise with them. If you feel embarrassed about asking other people to write things about you, you can use other ways to get this information from them. For example, you can tell your friends that you're doing a business exercise around your career options, and ask them what they think you're best at and why. Of course, you can ask them anything, in any way that you wish. Either way, the answers that come back to you will not only be enlightening, but they are also likely to cheer you up when you're feeling down.

If you prefer, you can even buy yourself a special journal in which to keep the things that people have said about you, or do it as an audio recording so that you can listen to it when you're feeling down!

Exercise

Exercise is a really powerful way to feel good. Your physical and mental states are intrinsically linked, so if your body feels good, your mind won't be able to help feeling good either. The more you move your body, the happier you're likely to feel. For those of you that like the yawn-y science part, the reason for this is that exercise releases chemicals in your brain known as endorphins. Simply put, endorphins are chemicals in the brain, which trigger happiness and relaxation. The more we can trigger these chemicals, the happier we will be. And who wouldn't want more happiness?

If the idea of going to the gym terrifies you, don't worry. Exercise can take a number of different forms. For example, if you love going out dancing, you could try going to a local salsa class or a club. Exercise could even be as simple as getting off your bus or train a stop early so that you have a longer walk, or spend time playing with your children. Exercise does not have to be a scary word, and in the process you'll feel better than ever.

Music

If I've completely failed to convince you with the exercise idea, the good news is that there's another way to release endorphins - music! Like exercise, music stimulates endorphins, as long as you pick a happy and uplifting track. If you like, try to remember the last time you went to hear live music, or went out to any sort of venue that played music. What kind of music makes you feel good? What are your favourite feel-good tracks? Add some of your favourites here to pick you up whenever you're feeling low:

....

....

....

Now that you have a playlist, lifting your mood can be as simple as playing your favourite song(s) in your car, or on your ipod!

Shay's Story

My favourite mood-boosting song at the moment is 'Never too Much' by Luther Vandross. Any time that I'm feeling down, I play the song in my car and make sure that I put my heart and soul into singing along to it. Admittedly, I am always by myself when this happens, so that I don't feel like a complete idiot. And no, despite my dabbling as a Jazz vocalist, I haven't been blessed with Aretha's voice either!

If you want to use this exercise at home, or maybe in one of your lonely corporate hotel rooms if you're away on work, you can also dance along to your song. If you use your body, as well as your voice, to appreciate the music that you're listening to, you're likely to feel even more of a mood boost. Remember that the best way to dance is as if no one is watching, and the best way to sing is to imagine no one is listening. The important thing is to enjoy the exercise, and of course no one need know that you have done this at all.

Don't stress about the bad small stuff, and instead, rejoice in the good small stuff.

Are you one of these people that get really upset when you

miss the train in the morning? Or perhaps by the time you get to your train station, your favourite newspaper has run out? One of the best things to do is to always put life's little irritations into perspective. By appreciating the little things in life that are good, and not stressing about the minor things in life that are bad, you will automatically improve your mood. You're alive, you're breathing, and you have food and a roof over your head – your reality is someone else's dream. Although not stressing is easier said than done, use this advice with the vision you created in your daydream, and hold onto that every time you catch yourself starting to feel stressed.

Have a Laugh

When is the last time that you had a really good laugh? Who were you with? What were you doing? Laughter is the best medicine in the world. As well as making you feel happier, laughter has health benefits too. The quality of your health is directly affected by how happy you are, and how much you laugh. Make sure that you fill your life with plenty of activities that will get you to laugh hard and heartily. The activity can be as simple as going to check out a live stand-up, hanging out with friends that make you laugh, or even just watching a comedy on TV. Take a moment now to think of a moment that made you laugh out loud; preferably one of those uncontrollable attacks of the giggles or a real belly laugh! Write your moment, or a selection of moments down here, so that you can always refer back to them when you're feeling down.

My 'Laugh Out Loud' Moments

....

....

....

Chapter Summary

- Always ask yourself quality questions
- Destroy your negative beliefs by finding more evidence for their empowering alternative
- Remember to adore yourself, be happy and love who you are by:
  Interpreting events positively
  Imagining yourself in gorgeous places
  Writing creatively
  Talking to yourself in the mirror
  Exercise
  Singing and dancing to your favourite songs
  Keeping things in perspective and stop stressing about the little things
  Laughing as often as you can

Chapter 2

"...but in the past...I can't wait til I'm..."
Knowing Where You Are Right Now

"Yesterday is history, tomorrow is a mystery, today is God's gift, that's why we call it the present"
Joan Rivers

Have you ever noticed that success attracts success, money attracts money and love attracts love? One very important part of being captivating is that you must be the best version of yourself that you possibly can. The more that you embody the most happy, gorgeous and self-confident version of your true self, the more magnetic, attractive and positively delicious you become. When you feel truly comfortable in your own skin, exuding the happiness and confidence that being the best 'you' can bring, the world can do nothing BUT be attracted to you and success and abundance will flow!

In order to get to this good and juicy stage, we are going to be looking at where you are now, so that you know what you need to do to get to the truly 'magnetic' state. One of the best places to start with this is to use the *'Wheel of Life'*.

A Wheel of Life is designed to show you how you're doing on the success barometer. It's essentially a snapshot of where you are in your life at the present moment. If you get a 10/10 in every category, then you're 100% successful! However, the person who gets 100% is probably 1 in a million! If you get a score of above 75%, then you're doing *really* well, and if you get a score between 55-75% then this would be fairly normal for the average, relatively happy person. If you have a score below this level, don't worry, it's very powerful to acknowledge where you are, so we can work together to make sure that you'll boost this score, and become that 1 in a million!

With my clients, I usually give them a blank wheel (as illustrated below) and ask them to identify what they see as being the ten most important areas of their life.

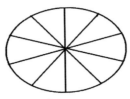

Imagine this circle is a wheel on a bike. Each spoke represents a different area of your life. At the very end of each spoke, write down which area of your life that it represents.

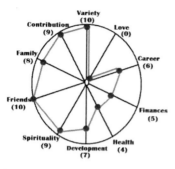

Fig 2 contains a worked example to help you create your own.

Once you've named each spoke, rate each area of your life on a scale of 0-10.

0 would represent you being a complete and utter mess about the issue, and nowhere near where you want to be, and 10 represents you being the utmost in perfection and completely fulfilled.

Figure 2 shows a worked example of a Wheel of Life. In this particular wheel, the person has chosen the areas that are most important to her and marked them on a scale of 1 to 10. When the dots have been joined up, you can see how circular, or how jagged a particular person's wheel is. The aim is for each person to have a smooth wheel, with each area of their life in balance. In the above example, you can see that the wheel is very jagged. This means, literally, that the person is having quite a bumpy ride in life at the moment.

Another interesting thing to do with the wheel, is to add up the scores in each area to get an overall score. If you add up all the scores above, the person in the example scores a total of 67%. This means that she is only 67% fulfilled in her life.

Each person, when leading an outstanding lifestyle, should aim to score between 85% and 100% on their wheel of life. This means, that she would automatically attract people and situations that are for her highest good and that are the very best. If you're living your life at 65% to 85%, on the whole you're probably doing okay and you would be attracting situations and people that are 'okay'. If you're living your life below 65%, then you immediately need to do some of the vision and purpose work in the next chapter to improve the quality of your life immediately. Once the quality of your own life starts to improve, the potential for success goes up exponentially.

Going back to the figure 2 example, the wheel is a simple way to show you which areas you need the most improvement in. For example, in this particular case, the areas of improvement that she needs to explore more are love, health, and finances.

Once you have completed the Wheel of Life, think of two minor changes in each of your lowest scoring areas that you could do in order to improve your score next time you do the Wheel of Life. Although it's important to make some changes, please make sure that you don't overburden yourself with a complete revamp if you're not ready to do so. A complete overhaul can cause a similarly imbalanced wheel next time around, so putting all your energies into your weakest areas means that some of your other areas may start to become affected in the process, and the overall score may actually go down.

You can use the table below to help you identify actions that you can take in order to help you boost your score. As you will notice, there is a column for time frame. This is because you're much more likely to do something if you have made a commitment to doing it in terms of time. I would, therefore, urge you all to schedule when you're identified actions will take place.

Area of Improvement	Actions I can take	Time frame
Love	1. I can ask my friends if there's anyone that they can set me up with.	1. I'll speak to Suzi about this on Saturday when we go out for dinner as she knows a lot of people.
	2. I can join a local drama class as I've always enjoyed acting and you never know who you could meet	2.I'll do a google search tonight to see what's available and give any potential classes a call tomorrow morning
Health	1. I'll go to the gym three times a week instead of twice a week.	1. I'll add Tuesday nights to my regular gym nights.
	2. I'll cook for myself rather than going out for dinner or getting take-aways all the time.	2. I'll do some food shopping on Monday night so I can cook for myself both then and on Wednesday evening.
Finances	1. I'll stop buying lunch everyday and make it at home.	Next Monday, as I'll be at the Supermarket anyway, I'll buy some stuff for both lunch and dinner.

In this case, each change that the person has made, moves her towards improving her entire life. Some of the changes that have been made, may even impact in more than one area. The key to your wheel is that it should always remain as balanced as possible.

Human Needs

An alternative way to look at your life is to use the human needs psychology theory put together by Tony Robbins. Each person will fulfill the first four needs, whether that is in a positive or negative way. However, to feel truly fulfilled, we must strive to fulfill all six of these human needs in a healthy way. These needs are:

The Basic Needs

1. Certainty
Simply put, certainty is like a comfort blanket. Certainty is our need to feel safe and secure. The healthiest way to achieve certainty is to have certainty within yourself, no matter what happens in your life. However, most people also feel safe or secure through the presence and actions of other people. Although this is very common, we must talk, so recognise that seeking certainty from others rather than ourselves, can often be very unhealthy.

Neville's Story

Leanne and Neville did everything together. Leanne led a fairly active social life, and had a very large group of friends. But, she always seemed to know where to go and what to do. Neville on the other hand did not have many friends outside of Leanne. As Neville saw it, Leanne was his "social secretary"! In other words, he relied on Leanne for his certainty around his social life, rather than feeling certain in who he was. Leanne eventually felt that Neville was being far too clingy and they fell out over it. Neville found this particularly hard, as he had never relied on himself to find certainty before.

2. Uncertainty

Uncertainty is God's way of playing games with our mind. Not only do we like the feeling of being secure and knowing what's going to happen, but we also feel that 'variety is the spice of life'. After all, if each day that we lived, was the same as the last, we would get very bored very quickly. Some people have a higher need for uncertainty than others, and it is a trait that is particularly common in entrepreneurs. In fact, it has also been said that the level of success that you will experience depends on the level of uncertainty that you're comfortable with. If you cling to certainty like your security blanket, you're likely to never take any risks or try new things. We should, therefore, all aim to be comfortable with a little uncertainty in our lives; it could lead to something even more magical than we ever dreamed of!

3. Significance

Don't you love it when you get complimented on a good piece of work? Or perhaps you've been told that you look really good today? Or maybe all the other parents think that you've raised the most wonderful children? Why do these comments and observations from others make us feel so good? Put simply, we also have a need for significance. We love to feel important!

As with certainty, the healthiest way to fulfil your need for significance is to feel significant within yourself, rather than seeking it from others and the outside world. Of course, getting compliments and feedback on how wonderful you are is always fantastic, but we should all have the talent to recognise, within ourselves, that we are already fantastic without having to have other people tell us in order to truly believe it.

4. Love and Connection

One of the deepest human fears is that we won't be loved. The need for love is very important within each human being. We all ultimately crave love, however, many people settle for just having a connection.

The need for love and connection can be fulfilled in unhealthy ways. For example, someone who suffers from depression may be satisfying their need for connection, as they are connecting with themselves on a deep emotional level. In contrast, a healthy way to meet the need for love and connection, is to always love and connect with yourself and in your relationships with others, do not settle for connection rather than love.

The Spiritual Needs

5. Growth

People always want to better their situations. In the healthiest minds, a person would want to learn more, give more, love more and generally always improve the quality of their life. The need for growth is, therefore, about developing yourself. If you're not on a journey where you're developing yourself in some way, you'll feel stagnant and very unfulfilled.

6. Contribution

Life is always better when it is shared. Contribution is about magnifying your good feelings by helping others to feel good too, and making the world a better place in general.

Once you have understood these six human needs, you can use your understanding of them to analyse where you are in your life. Use the human needs table below to analyse how well your needs are being met in each area of your life:

Area of Improvement	Actions I can Take	Timeframe

To fill in the table, ask yourself the following question for each box:

On a scale of 1 to 10 how well is my need for (*insert need here*) being met in relation to (*insert area of life here*)?"

1 represents being a complete and utter failure, where the particular need is not being met in any way, shape or form and 10 represents fulfilling your needs at the highest level you can possibly achieve.

Once you have completed the human needs table, you will see which areas of your life are fulfilling your unique needs the most and which areas need the most work.

You could also try this exercise with a partner and analyse how well you're meeting each other's needs in your relationship. If you're in a relationship, it is particularly interesting to do this exercise together so that you can find out where you both are in each area of your lives, and you know in which areas you need to support each other.

Human needs psychology can help us to understand why we do what we do, and once analysed in this way, it can help us create major shifts in our life by fulfilling our human needs in other ways. When a particular behaviour fulfills three or more of the human needs, the behaviour will become an addiction. The way to conquer this is to find an alternative behaviour that meets your need with a higher score and perhaps leads to other people supporting you once you know where your areas of weakness are.

Minnie's Story

Minnie is a very successful business woman. She had a great job, a lovely home and a wonderful fiancé who completely adored her. Yet there was something missing, but, she couldn't quite tap into what. I shared the human needs psychology theory with Minnie. Within the session, she realised what was missing...the feeling of being significant.

Things had got so routine at work especially, that she just didn't feel very important any more. By identifying her need for significance, she was able to address the situation with her boss, as well as sharing her feelings with her fiancé who supported her brilliantly.

Chapter Summary

- You must always strive to be at your happiest.
- Knowing where you are right now is a very powerful tool for you to be able to measure the level of improvement needed. It can also be particularly encouraging to know where you were initially once you start to make improvements.
- Fill in the Wheel of Life to show how smooth your ride in life is at the moment.
- If you're in for a bumpy ride, write down, and follow through with at least two actions that you can undertake in order to boost your Wheel of Life score.
- Also, fill in the human needs psychology exercise in order to see where you could be meeting your needs better.

Chapter 3

"It's a man's world – but it don't mean nothing without a woman"
Living in Your Core Masculine and Feminine Energy

"One of the best metaphors for a woman living primarily in her masculine energy and a man living primarily in his feminine energy is to image what happens when you put batteries into your remote control the wrong way around. Nothing! The zing is only there when the batteries go around the right way; opposites attract!"
Tony and Nicki Vee

Men and women are different. I know... Newsflash!

Think about it though, the things that make a man feel good are different from the things that make a woman feel good. No matter what the feminist movement may think, there are a lot of women who still like to feel taken care of, protected and cherished, no matter how independent they are in their job and in their life. And no matter what a man thinks, there is still a part of him that wants to be the caveman hunter-gatherer who is able to look after his woman properly!

In our society, the Dalai Lama obviously felt that without one battery turned towards the feminine, the remote control of the world doesn't quite work! At the Vancouver Peace Summit 2009, he is quoted as saying that *'the world would be saved by the Western Woman.'* He seems to recognise the need for feminine energy in the world, to give it a good spring clean, and magically rid it of all its problems to bring us back to a place of beauty and harmony.

So all this is interesting, but how on earth do you use it in your own life? And how on earth does this make us magnetic and captivating? Well, as with living in the happiest, best version of yourself, living in your core feminine energy makes you *immediately* captivating. Opposites DO attract, so play to your strengths. Take Marilyn Monroe as an example. No matter what you may think of her, you can't deny that she oozed femininity, it was one of the reasons that she became so captivating to both men and women.

What we are going to do now is look at your core energy. Are you more masculine or feminine? Which side should you work with in order to ensure instant magnetism?

Have a look at the following list, which contains a number of traits. For each trait, rate them on a scale of 1 to 7 using the following scale:

1 = Never or almost never true
2 = Usually not true
3 = Sometimes but infrequently true
4 = Occasionally true

5 = Often true

6 = Usually true

7 = Always or almost always true

Remember to rate each trait as honestly as you can:

Column A	Column B	Column C
Cheerful	Self reliant	Tender
Tactful	Defends own beliefs	Sympathetic
Affectionate	Independent	Sensitive to other's needs
Open to flattery	Competitive	Compassionate
Shy	Assertive	Eager to soothe hurt feelings
Emotional	Strong personality	Soft spoken

Column D	Column E	Column F
ambitious	expressive	dominant
analytical	nurturing	initiative
leadership ability	intuitive	willing to take a stand
willing to take risks	loves children	aggressive
makes decisions easily	gentle	acts as a leader
self-sufficient	sociable	individualistic

Once you've scored each of the above traits, add up the total score in each column. You can record your results here:

TOTALS:

COLUMN A
COLUMN B
COLUMN C
COLUMN D
COLUMN E
COLUMN F

Now add the following: (1) $A + C + E =$
                        (2) $B + D + F =$
Lastly subtract: $(1) - (2) =$

This is what your scores mean:

Score	Meaning
< -20	Very Feminine
-19 to -10	Somewhat Feminine
-9 to 0	Neutral
-9 to -10	Somewhat Masculine
-19 > -20	Masculine

The quiz starts to give you an idea of whether you're operating largely in masculine or feminine energy. The list below also gives you an idea of some common masculine and feminine traits:

Masculine	Feminine
Strong	Gentle
Provider	Nurturer
Aggressive	Sensitive
Assertive	Sympathetic
Logical	Intuitive
Homemaker	Homebuilder
Go getting	Allowing
Quiet	Outspoken
Ambitious	Passive
Family and inwardly orientated	Socially and outwardly orientated
Initiative	Responsive
Competitive	Cooperative
Risk taker	emotional
Dominance	Submission
Authority	Power (to bring people/elements together)

As you can see, both masculine and feminine traits have their strengths. In today's society, however, it is masculine traits that have been given the most prominence, and women as well as men have been encouraged to develop these. Consider Clarissa's story as a cautionary tale for girls that operate primarily in the masculine.

Clarissa's Story

Do you remember the Wizard of Oz? All throughout the film, we had an image of the Wizard being big, scary and imposing. When we got to the end of the film, we realise that the Wizard is an unimposing, mild mannered guy who is not scary in the least. He is simply hiding behind a threatening smokescreen. Well, this reminded me of Clarissa and Steve. I hardly ever manage to speak to Steve when I talk to them as he appears to be controlled by his own threatening smokescreen – Clarissa! Steve is a very mild mannered, gentle and charming individual, but you don't get to meet or speak to him in a business context at all without going through Clarissa first.

Clarissa's story is sadly very familiar in many relationships. Now reverse the names in the story, and read it again. How much better would it feel if Steve were the protector (in a healthy way of course) and Clarissa was the mild mannered one being looked after by her husband? I know I'm in danger of sounding like a 1950's housewife, but I'm not, I am an intelligent 21st Century Woman who is being honest. Be honest with yourself – on a deeper level, what do you really prefer? Remember the story as a moral as to what could happen if women start behaving entirely like men, and men start behaving entirely like women.

Ladies, don't be afraid to use your feminine power even if you're a 21st century girl who is able to make your own living, in fact especially if you're a 21st century woman. Don't be afraid to use your intuition, to nurture others around you and to act with wisdom, listening to the advice of your heart as well as your head. Feminine energy is externally focused, so the easiest way to develop the feminine side of you is to develop a deep belief in the value of the life of others, and focus on doing what is right and good. And sometimes, this even means not being afraid to let go, rather than obsessively trying to control everything around you. As metro-sexual as a lot of men are these days, there's still a caveman lurking just below the surface. Most men still occasionally wants to perform their 'hunter-gatherer' role, so becoming the big feminist and refusing his help with everything financial, for instance, is more likely to frighten him off, as he'll end up not seeing a role for himself and feel like there's no need to stay around. He just needs to know that although you're capable of doing things for yourself, you're letting him help, be there for you and support you. If you're a single girl, don't pretend that you have it *all* sussed and that you don't need anyone; any man who comes into your life will want to be able to add to it in a positive way, so make sure you leave some room for him.

We have all become experts in displaying our masculine traits. I am obviously completely okay with women in the workplace; I am also in favour of making sure that women don't forget that they're women. We should be just as proud to use the feminine energy that is within us, as we are of our self-sufficiency – both energies are just as important as the other. Sometimes, we're so good at embracing our masculine characteristics, that we can be much better at it than the men in our lives! However funny this appears on the surface, it is actually quite a sad observation that places us in great danger in terms of our own fulfillment. Living in your opposite energy will never feel quite right or comfortable and will affect every area of your life, from how you behave at work, to what kind of relationships you'll attract into your life.

For the Guys

I suggest leaving this page open for the men in your life…

Men, I know you've been having a tough time. I know it looks like the girls are completely able to look after themselves now, and that you don't really know what to do with yourself. The easiest way to develop the strength of your masculinity is to just take control, and foster a deep belief in the value of your own life. Focus on your purpose, and what you'd like to achieve, and be in control of that. This will not only make you feel better, but will inevitably also make you more attractive to the women around you. When it comes to relating to women in general, remember, inside every woman, no matter how good she is at living in a man's world, is a girl that wants to be able to look to you for strength and protection.

So step up to the challenge. Show her that you have confidence in yourself and you're able to protect and provide for her no matter what. Don't lose your confidence and let your woman do it all. Without a purpose in your own life, you'll begin to feel very unfulfilled and may not even know what is wrong. The more you live in your masculine energy, the more happy and fulfilled you'll start to feel in yourself.

Nathan's Story

Nathan is a typical example of the 21st Century man – CONFUSED! He is told that he needs to be politically correct and that women are his equal. He accepts this. He's been told off in the past for holding doors open for women, offering them his coat if they are cold and paying for meals, because the women he meets are perfectly capable of looking after themselves.

What he did not realise (before talking to me, of course), was that as a man, it is his innate nature to want to look after a woman. In being a 'gentleman', some 21st Century ladies have made him feel 'wrong' for this behaviour. The sad thing is, if these ladies were to also embrace the innate feminine within them, their core truth would almost certainly be that they would enjoy this level of care and attention.

Nathan's story really highlighted to me how both sexes are confused about their innate natural tendencies. I realise this may be a little controversial. I'm not afraid to share that when I first started exploring this subject, I found the idea quite unpalatable myself. As a woman who was determined to make it on my own, I found the idea of letting a man look after me and take care of my needs quite abhorrent. However, when I examined my *own* truth, I learned how to embrace my femininity, and over the years, I have discovered that it has been far more powerful than being a woman who behaves like a man. It has also changed the type of men I have attracted. In the past, I have attracted men that want me to protect them, but the more I embrace my feminine core, the more the quality of both my personal and professional relationships improve. And none of this involved letting go of my intelligence, confidence and ambition.

Exploring our differences helps us to learn how to support each other and ultimately, how to bring out the best in each other. When men and women in their correct energy come together, that is when you get true polarity, and, therefore, the strongest attraction between the sexes. For same sex couples, the study of masculine and feminine energies is nevertheless brilliant in helping you to understand your own sex and how to relate to them better. At the end of the day, we're all equal, but our qualities are different, so play to both your strengths and your partner's strengths for an ideal balance.

Chapter Summary

- Make sure that you're living in your core feminine energy.
- Don't be afraid to use feminine energy – although it may not be "the norm" in today's society, even the Dalai Lama thinks it's fabulous!
- Attraction explodes to unbelievable heights when you're willing to live in your core energy and helps you to achieve true fulfillment.

Chapter 4

"I don't know what I want!"
Life is a Blank Canvas – Paint Your Dreams onto It!

"You've got to follow your passion. You've got to figure out what it is you love – who you really are. And have the courage to do that. I believe that the only courage anybody ever needs is the courage to follow your own dreams"
Oprah Winfrey

I'm going to ask you to venture into your imagination and let yourself dare to wish for your wildest dreams. Throughout my life, I have found that being in touch with my dreams not only makes me 100 times more likely to achieve them, but having vision helps me to be perceived as exciting and inspirational, as opposed to having nothing better to talk about than what's going on in the latest TV soap.

So, let's get in touch with your dreams. A great place to start is to imagine that you're 90 years old. You're probably sitting on your porch, reflecting on what life has been like. When you've pictured the scene, think about the following questions:

- What would the 90-year-old version of you want to be telling yourself?
- If you were writing your autobiography, what would you want to be able to say?
- What do you want to have achieved?
- Who do you want in your life?
- What aspects of your life would you be the most proud of?

Thinking of our lives in this way, often gives us a good idea of what we want to achieve in our lives.

If you know what you want, you're more likely to get it. Knowing what you want not only sharpens your focus so that you work towards achieving your dream, but you'll also be more open to noticing opportunities, signs or just funny little coincidences which are going to help you along the way.

Shay's Car Story

I usually compare the results of focusing your mind on something to car buying. I recently bought a little Toyota IQ, which I'd intended to buy for the last few months. When I was out driving, if you'd asked me how many Toyota IQs I noticed on my journey, I could probably have told you as I was actively seeking them. On the other hand, if you asked me how many Peugeot 206s I noticed, I wouldn't be able to tell you that at all. As I had the idea of buying a Toyota IQ in my head, my mind was more open to noticing them on the road, and eventually, yes, I did buy one!

So, knowing what you want can lead you to getting a car; maybe

I should have wished for a Porsche! Seriously though, if you dare to dream it, you can make it a reality.

Okay so let's have some fun by starting with defining what you want!

The Wish Board

For those of you that are really creative, or just like to go back to doing the things we did when we were 7 years old, you're going to love this exercise. Start by going to your local art shop and getting yourself a very large sheet of paper and whatever else you may want to be creative with. Also have a rummage through your magazines and newspapers at home.

Once you have some creative materials around you, spend the next few hours in total indulgence, finding your favourite pictures in the magazines and drawing representations of things that you like. If you're good at drawing, you can create what you wish, or if you're technically minded you can even use the computer and images that you find online. The result is a 'wish-board' representing who you are and what you want in your life. Below is an example of one I created cutting out clippings from magazines:

As you can see, all I did in this image is use clippings and words to represent things that I wanted in my life. If you want to use the

Feng Shui method of creating a vision, as I have done, use the following grid to organise the pictures that you have, and stick them in the appropriate areas.

Once you have created your wish board, remember to put it somewhere prominent so that you're always reminded of your vision and it remains fresh in your mind.

The last time I did this exercise, I took the idea a step further by doing it in a book rather than as an actual collage. I filled each page with aspirations around different areas of my life, both in crayon pictures and in collage form. As I love to write, I also wrote some things on each page that also represented what I wanted.

Whilst we're on the subject of writing, if you prefer the written word to visual imagery, you can create a written, rather than a visual representation, of what you want. Or of course you can do both like I did. A written representation can be done in one of three ways:

The Shopping List

This is probably the best idea for those of you that don't like too much creative writing. Each time we go to the supermarket, many of us make a list of what we want. Once we're at the supermarket, the list makes it easier for us to go to the right places to find each of those things.

As with the visual idea, take a few hours of total indulgence for this one and let your imagination run away with you. Focus on those things that you truly desire. If you want to make it really detailed, use the categories that you chose for your wheel of life in the last chapter and write a list of things that would make that area of your life perfect. As I said, if you dare to dream, it's much more likely to come to you. The scariest place to be is not knowing what you want, and to let life run away with you.

If this seems too hard right now, you can also start by writing down what you don't want and use the opposites of that to create your wish list. If you do start with the negatives, remember to take a break before you get onto the positives so that you're in the right state of mind when you start doing the wish list.

If you're stuck, you can, of course, discuss this with your friends and family to help you define what it is that you want. However, a word of caution, if you do get help with this, remember that ultimately this is *your* list and *your* wishes to make *you* happy. You're the only person who truly knows what makes you happy – not your friends and family.

Make the list as long as you like; the most important aspect of this list is the detail in it. The more you ask for, the more you'll get, so don't be shy or feel too greedy about the whole thing – just get wishing!

Writing Your Future Life Story

If you're a bit of a writer, you'll love doing this. If visuals or lists don't do it for you, cast your mind back to when your English teacher used to tell you to write creative stories at school. If you're anything like me (and I realise that as a straight A English student I may be in the minority here), you were filled with excitement at the prospect of creating something amazing!

Again, you can split the story into sections and write a section for each area of your life based on the categories that you used in your wheel, or just using the titles of my chapters in the *attract* section of this book. You can use the following questions to get you started on your creative journey. Remember to ask yourself these questions by imagining that you've already got what you want:

- What's my ideal "everyday" day? What am I going to be doing in it?
- What will I do to maintain my perfect health on a daily basis?

- Who is in my life at the moment?
- What is my love life like? Am I in a relationship or married? Do I have children? – How did I meet my partner?
- What is my interaction like with everyone in my family?
- How much time do I spend with my family?
- What do I do for a living? How many hours a week do I work? How did I get into my job?
- Where do I live? What is my home like?
- Who are my friends? How often do I see them?
- What do I do socially?
- How does living my perfect life make me feel?

Make the piece of writing as detailed as you like – the more detailed it is, the better!

Once you've written either your list, or your creative writing piece, revisit them often – preferably every day. Add details to them when you re-read them, and delete any details you no longer want. By staying focused on your desires, you're more likely to draw them to you, and by reading them everyday, your desires will stay fresh in your mind at all times.

Incantations

So what exactly are incantations? The word 'incant' actually comes from a Latin word, which means 'to cast a magic spell.' In modern terms, incantations are statements you say to yourself everyday in order to keep your desires fresh in your mind. They must be positive, powerful and written in words that mean something to you. They must also be easy for you to remember. If you've done one of the other exercises, you can start by picking out the words from the exercise that most resonate with you.

Below are a few examples of short incantations to get you started. However, your incantation should encapsulate every-thing that is most important to you and be written in your own words:

"I am a money magnet, and prosperity of all kinds is drawn to me"

"I am a world class (insert career) and the world appreciates my natural gift of (insert quality)"

"I naturally make choices that are good for me, I take loving care of my body and my body responds with health, an abundance of energy and a wonderful feeling of well-being"

"My work is enjoyable and fulfilling, and I am appreciated"

"I make friends easily wherever I go"

"I attract men easily with my wit, style and intelligence. I find conversations with the opposite sex effortless"

"All I need is within me now"

"All my relationships are harmonious, happy and serve my highest good"

Have a go at writing some of your own incantations here:

....

....

....

Once you've written your incantation, how do you use them? And what if you don't believe your incantation yet? Well, there are a number of ways you can say them to yourself. Many people like to use the bathroom mirror in the morning and say their incantation to themselves then. I prefer to switch of my brain entirely and say them to myself when I'm at the gym in the mornings. That way, my body and brain is engaged in movement whilst I am saying my incantation. No one needs to know that you're saying them, especially if you don't feel confident enough to say them out loud at the gym or on your run, but having your body engaged while you're doing them helps your brain to switch off any doubt that your incantation isn't true, as its too busy thinking about movement. It's a clever little way to get that incantation into your subconscious and, therefore, into your reality!

Another way to tackle any doubts, is to form your incantations as questions, e.g. 'How are all my relationships happy and harmonious?' Your brain will then be too busy trying to find an answer to your question rather than throwing up doubts about its truth.

The more you believe something about yourself and the more you visualise or repeat it, the more likely it is to happen. Before long, you'll be acting out those new behaviours and attracting those new experiences as if they were always there.

Rose's Story

Rose was buying a house with her husband. When she had been a child, she had driven past a particular house on the English coast that she absolutely adored. In fact it was one of the most beautiful houses there.

Children are much more open to daring to dream. Rose's dream was that she would one day live in that very house. And when it came to buying a house, guess which house came onto the market at that very time? Rose ended up living in the house of her dreams!

If you can inadvertently create your future home just by randomly daydreaming as a child, imagine what you can do when you focus your thoughts and create the life that you *really* want?!

Lastly on this, remember to take as long as you need. Creating the rest of your life is a very important process. Do all the exercises in this chapter, or just one – whichever works for you. Whatever you choose to do, I would recommend taking at least 4 hours minimum to put this together, if not a 24-hour period where you just take the day and night off, and dedicate yourself to the task of putting your dreams together. Then, all you need to do is revisit it often and keep an eye out for the unexpected help that comes your way to get you to your dream!

Chapter Summary

- Imagine that you're 90 years old and looking back on your life. What do you want to be looking back on?
- Get hold of some old newspapers and magazines and make a collage of all the things that represent what you want for your life. You can also draw these out. Once you're done, put it in a place of prominence so that you're always reminded of it.
- Write either a list or a story about your ideal life and look at it often, making any changes that are necessary
- Once you have defined what you want, write a short incantation in your own words that you can say to yourself everyday to help create the life you desire.
- If you dare to dream, your dream is so much more likely to come to you.

Chapter 5

"If it wasn't for THEM, I'd be a HUGE success"
The Power of Adoring the World (no matter what it's done to you!)

"Tolerance, openness and understanding towards other peoples' cultures, social structures, values and faiths are now essential to the very survival of an interdependent world."
Aga Khan IV

Before we go on to how to be captivating with your looks, one last key to ultimate success is to remember to not just adore yourself, but others, and the world around you. Two of our most basic emotional needs are connection and contribution. The healthiest way to fulfill these is to connect with, and befriend others, and contribute to your society in a meaningful way – after all, it's no good adoring yourself and never stepping outside to greet the world, is it?

The reason why I love the quote by The Aga Khan is that we, as human beings, find it easy to spend time being negative about others – sometimes without even knowing a thing about them! On a world level, this sort of attitude towards others will never get you anywhere in life as you never know who you're going to upset with the prejudice that you dish out. On a more selfish level, we all have a certain amount of energy within us that can be converted into either something good, or something bad. Instead of focusing on the bad stuff, why not use the finite energy that you have, to just give out love and the good stuff? Not only will you feel a lot better, but you'll get a much better reaction from the people around you, and as a consequence, the rest of the world.

Many writers such as Deepak Chopra and Brendan Bays amongst others, have taken the negative energy theory even further and gone as far as stating that such negativity can turn into adverse affects on your body and health in general. If you're unable to deal with the emotional issues and anger, you run the risk that the pain you feel may manifest itself in another way. An easy example of this is imagining people who are highly stressed. They usually also suffer from high blood pressure due to the tense emotions that they frequently feel. Further down the line, it can also have effects on your immune system and lead to long-term illnesses. We all have the choice to think about good things or bad things; the more good things we fill our minds with, the more we're helping both our bodies and minds to stay in peak health.

In fact, the philosophical concept of causality actually goes as far as saying:

We cause every event in our life to happen.

Have a think about the power of that statement. Often, it is the easiest thing in the world to blame someone else for the bad things that have happened to us. In fact, the concept is so powerful it is actually one of the fundamental principles under-pinning Buddhism, particularly when you consider their views on Karma. Let's have a think about what happens when you blame someone else? What does blame actually do? Sometimes, there may be incidents, as in Jena's example, that seem easier to blame on someone else.

Jena's Story

Jena was jealous of a woman who appeared to be attracted to her boyfriend, Chris. She could not get her feelings of inadequacy out of her head. The feeling festered up inside her to the point where she feared losing Chris. As she wasn't in a good place emotionally, she started treating him in ways that indicated that she was jealous of the other woman. The episode culminated in Chris having an affair with the other woman – the very thing that Jena had feared the most.

To the outside world and to Jena herself, it's easy to blame Chris for his affair. However, how would it be if Jena took responsibility for her actions and accepted that it was her jealously and lack of trust that caused her to experience this situation in her life? Yes, this may sound harsh, but the one thing you can do to improve future situations, is to accept responsibility for your past ones and learn from these. When we hand over responsibility for the events in our life to outside sources and other people, we become powerless. Taking responsibility for everything that we say and do – even if we don't want to – puts us in a position of absolute power to design the life that we desire and create the results that we want.

Another lesson to be taken from Jena's story is the power of negative emotions, and how much they can destroy you. Nelson Mandela summed this up beautifully by saying that *'Resentment*

is like drinking poison and then hoping it will kill your enemies.'
The remedy for this is to forgive where you can, and at the very
least, to make peace with yourself if you cannot.

Forgiveness is our mastery over our own emotional pain and
can be one of the most powerful things that you can do to set
yourself free. Of course I am not saying that you should tolerate
behaviour that is bad or oppressive, but don't let it rule your life.
Yes, someone may have treated you badly. If that is the case, why
make them a priority in your mind by thinking about how much
they have angered you? Instead, it's better to set you free by using
a forgiveness process and to feel true peace within yourself. This
is not for the benefit of the other person or to condone their
behaviour in any way, but to allow you the gift of peace by not
harbouring the negative emotion anymore.

If you have experienced a disconnection with someone, try the
technique below to make peace within your subconscious – once
you have healed your inner self with the forgiveness process, the
outer you will probably be a lot more relaxed and at peace.

Forgiveness Process

1. Close your eyes, and for a few seconds picture the person
   who's hurt you. Let all your negative emotions come up. As
   you do this, notice the feelings that you're feeling in your
   body such as rising tensions, quickening heartbeat and
   shallow breathing. Promise yourself that you do not want
   to feel these emotions again.
2. Now light a candle and focusing on the flickering flame. If
   you don't have a candle, close your eyes and imagine a
   candle flame in front of you.
3. Let yourself take some deep breaths. As you breathe in,
   imagine that you're breathing in plus signs, and as you
   breathe out, imagine that you're breathing out minus signs.
   As you breathe, you'll notice that your body will automatically feel more positive and the negativity will be drained

out of your body.

4. Once you feel your body filling up with positivity and calm, start to picture yourself in a beautiful place with someone who supports you and that you trust. This person can be someone you know, someone imaginary, God, an older version of you or anything or anyone you feel has the wisdom to guide you. Let your mind fill itself with the joy, peace and beauty that this person and this place brings you.

5. Now, imagine that the warm feelings you're feeling from the place and from the person supporting you are like a smoky, protective shield. Imagine that the feeling is flooding you from within and creating a protective barrier around you, so that no negativity is allowed to penetrate it. Allow the barrier to soothe you and let it protect you.

6. When you feel safe in that place, with your barrier around you, imagine that the person that you've experienced a disconnect with has come to that place. From the most loving part of you, say what you need to say to them, including all those things that can't be said. Don't hold back – this is your chance to have that conversation! Ask your chosen guide from step 3 to help you if you need them.

7. Now imagine the most beautiful, loving, part of *them*. Underneath all that ego, what would the purest part of their soul say to you in response to what you've just told them? Have that conversation now. Take as long as you need to finalise the conversation.

8. Once you've finished having the conversation, ask yourself if you're willing to forgive that person; not to condone what they did, but to give yourself freedom from feeling that negativity.

9. Finish the exercise by taking a few last deep breaths, keeping the protective barrier around you and breathing

the good feelings that you feel into you. Now take a look again at the person you're angry at. Let the good feelings protect you. The purpose of doing this step is to break the pattern of stress reactions that normally occur in your mind and body when you think of the person who hurt you. When you surround your heart with positive energy, the power the person has had over you begins to dissipate.

Resentment is a habit, and habits take roughly twenty-five days to change. So if you do this exercise each time you think of the person who hurt you over twenty-five days, you will literally change your mental and physical reactions. They will no longer have power to hurt you, because you will have reprogrammed your own reactions. And when this happens, you start to become free.

I'd like to end this chapter with a story that came through my inbox today, as if it was just meant to be added here! It's a beautiful illustration of the power that our actions have on others and that the responsibility of creating what's around you is in your hands.

One Glass of Milk

One day, a poor boy who was selling goods from door to door to pay his way through school, found he had only one thin dime left, and he was hungry.

He decided he would ask for a meal at the next house. However, he lost his nerve when a lovely young woman opened the door.

Instead of a meal he asked for a drink of water! She thought he looked hungry so brought him a large glass of milk. He drank it so slowly, and then asked, 'How much do I owe you?'

'You don't owe me anything,' she replied. 'Mother has taught us never to accept pay for a kindness.'

He said ... 'Then I thank you from my heart.'

Howard Kelly had been ready to give up and quit, but as he left that house, he felt physically and emotionally stronger, with his faith in God and mankind restored.

Many years later the young woman became critically ill. The local doctors were baffled. They finally sent her to the big city, where they called in specialists to study her rare disease.

Dr. Howard Kelly was called in for the consultation. When he heard the name of the town she came from, a strange light filled his eyes. Immediately he rose and went down the hall of the hospital to her room.

Dressed in his doctor's gown he went in to see her. He recognized her at once.

He went back to the consultation room determined to do his best to save her life. From that day he gave special attention to her case.

After a long struggle, the battle was won.

Dr. Kelly requested the business office to pass the final bill to him for approval. He looked at it, wrote something on the edge, and the bill was sent to her room. She feared to open it, for she was sure it would take the rest of her life to pay for it all. Finally she looked, and something caught her attention on the side of the bill. She read these words...

'Paid in full with one glass of milk'

(Signed) Dr. Howard Kelly.

Tears of joy flooded her eyes as her happy heart prayed: 'Thank You God that your love has spread broad through human hearts and hands.'

There's a saying that goes something like this: Bread cast on the water comes back to you. The good deed you do today may benefit you or someone you love at the least expected time. If you never see the deed again at least you will have made the world a better place – and, after all, isn't that what life is all about?

If you follow the path to becoming a captivating presence, success is destined to follow you. Part of this success is going to be due to others' support of you, so don't forget them on your journey. When you start attracting absolute abundance, it's very important to not forget who got you there in the first place. Your clients, friends and family allow you to have the type of life that you're living, and contribute to your success, love, finances and just about everything, so never forget them and let go of any negativity that you may be feeling. It won't serve you on your journey and you're the only person who has chosen to feel that way.

Chapter Summary

- Connection and Contribution are two significant needs that each person feels.
- We have a choice to think positive or negative things about others and the world around us. Filling our minds with the negative can have adverse affects on our health, but filling our minds with the positive can truly create abundance.
- We reap what we sow. When we are in a place where we can take responsibility for our feelings, actions and events around us, we become truly powerful.
- Forgiveness is a tool that can set you free from negativity. I'm not advocating being a walkover, but I am advocating filling your mind with only the things that are worthwhile.

PART 2

BEING CAPTIVATING: THE LOOK

What is a flower?
At Weddings, people bring flowers
At births, people bring flowers
On special occasions, people bring flowers
And at funerals people bring flowers
Why?
Flowers are beautiful, strong and constant, no matter what the
*   occasion.*
Life like a flower; always radiating the beauty and constancy
*   that they bring, no matter what the occasion.*
Saquina Sacoor Ahmed

Chapter 6

"What on earth do I wear?!"
Dress to Impress

"Clothes can suggest, persuade, connote, insinuate, or indeed lie, and apply subtle pressure while their wearer is speaking frankly and straightforwardly of other matters."
Anne Hollander

Now, if you're not a fan of clothes, you may be thinking at this point, that your skills, your intelligence and sense of humour are more than enough to win someone over. You may think that society's importance on looks is a complete waste of time because you're beyond that, and people should like you just for you.

You're absolutely right. People *should* like you just for you. However, if you ignore something as simple as getting the way that you dress right, you may be making things a lot more difficult for yourself. It may be okay to look like a mess if you're in a grungy pop band, but if you choose to take that to business, people will be more likely to notice your lack of dress sense before you get the chance to show off your intelligence and finesse in your industry. It always helps to make the most of what you already have. After all, the way that you present yourself is your passport to having a deeper connection with people that you meet. Unfortunately, people are judgmental. 40% of the population is primarily visually driven. That is quite a large percentage of the population to not connect with, just because you don't want to make an effort with clothing.

Persuaded that this is more than just a bit of fun? Good.

Being stylish is not about being dressed head-to-toe in the latest Vivienne Westwood creation – it's more about being comfortable in what you wear and carrying it off beautifully with your attitude. Start by thinking about what the happiest, most successful, best version of you would like to wear. If you're in last week's grubby denim jeans, are you really reflecting your inner message and showing people what you're all about in the first few seconds? Think about what type of person you are and how you wish to express that to the world. If you prefer, you can think about what type of person you would like to be and what style of clothes you think that person would be wearing. Then dress for the personality that you actually want to exude. Spending a few minutes tapping into what you *really* want to look like before you start shopping, can make a world of difference.

Connie's Story

Connie is a confident individual who likes to be noticed. Her clothes help her to express this and to feel more confident about herself. She is feminine, educated and sophisticated, and this comes across in the way she dresses. She often says a confident person is not afraid of confident items of clothing, such as hats or bolder colours.

Now she wear things that emphasise her personality and her wardrobe is full of items that are feminine, elegant, but that stand out a little too. She describes one of her favourite outfits as being a polka dot vintage dress, which she wears with contrasting boots and understated jewellery. This look is not going to work for everyone, but it works for her as she feels it emphasises her personality and it gets her noticed which is something that she likes. She even gets compliments on her clothes from people who would never dress like her because she carries them off so well and it's a look that works for her. The tip here is to dress for the personality that you have, or want to have.

Dress for your Business Personality

Clothes are an expression of you and your business! If you have a bold personality, this can be expressed by wearing bold colours or prints. If for example, you wish you had a bold personality, bold clothes can help you to feel this way and adopt this attitude. Clothes can also be an expression of your mood. For example, a woman in a romantic mood may opt to wear something pink or floral to express that mood through her clothing.

It is vital that you reflect the business that you're in at all times.

Wendy's Story

Take for example my client Wendy. Wendy runs holistic retreats for women promoting health, vitality and a passion for life. In her old business photo on the left, Wendy could have easily been mistaken for a friendly city worker. Following some work with me, we recreated Wendy's business image. She now uses the picture on the right for her business, reflecting the vitality and the joy for

life that she wanted to portray in her business.

If you get this tip absolutely right, you can easily have potential clients and people coming to you rather than you having to do all the hard work to get noticed!

Dress for the Occasion

Different times in your business may call for different looks to be used.

Jolene's Story

Jolene is a TV producer, presenter, author and intuitive, with a mission to bring spiritually conscious living to a wider society. The picture on the left was taken in Glastonbury, embracing her spiritual side. However, when she came to see me, she was about to follow a media path in LA. The look on the right was, therefore, more powerful and professional, suiting the LA image that Jolene wanted to portray at that time.

Dress for Your Physique

This is a mistake many people make. They see something that looks nice on a shop rail and decide that they must instantly own it without considering whether this item would actually look good on them. Clothes should accentuate your positive features. If, for example, you have perfect legs, you may want to show them off with skinny or fitted jeans, or for the ladies, a short skirt. Tailored clothing or anything that shows off your best bits, may work for the more curvaceous woman.

Don't be Afraid to Use Control Underwear

Ok, so control underwear isn't exactly uber-sexy looking, but it can make your whole outfit look much sexier where it is needed. There are very few of us that would consider ourselves as having the perfect figure, so instead of stressing about those few extra pounds, lack of muscle definition on your tummy or thunder thighs, check out the control underwear section next time you go shopping and it could very easily become your new best friend.

For a little bit of extra help and curves to make Dita Von Teese jealous, you could also consider purchasing a corset. Corsets can reduce your waist size by up to 4 inches whilst still remaining comfortable to wear, although I would not recommend them for everyday use. If you have the budget, go for steel boning so that it always retains its shape. Some of them even make fabulous over-wear.

Show Skin Strategically

Although you should absolutely dress for your physique, for the more confident amongst you, don't overdo it – you don't want to look trashy. A great rule to go by is to pick one area and show it off, but no more than that. For women, the classic rule is not to do a low cut top AND a mini skirt. For men, I see very few of you in breach of this rule.

If you're buying a few items of clothing at the same time, barter with the assistant – even if it is a store rather than a market. Many high street and designer stores still have employees working on commission. If you want to buy more than one item of clothing, or several accessories, it's worth asking whether there could be a discount applied. One person I know even takes it as far as using a bit of harmless flirtation in the buying process, then asking for a discount at the end. It often works and it just goes to show, that it never hurts to ask. If you want some more tips on how to build that connection with someone, flick over to chapter

15 to get you started or of course, my book *'The Grown Up Guide to Kiss Chase'* will have you flirting like a pro if that's a skill you want to develop further!

Chrissy's Story

Chrissy and I found the ideal dress for her soulmate manifestation business. Unfortunately it was about £70 over budget on a rail in the heart of Kings Road, Chelsea – one of the most expensive shopping streets in London. However, by engaging a few of my bargaining skills, we managed to get the dress within Chrissy's budget and it has now become part of her business brand.

If You're Buying Suits, Shop Around for Corporate Discounts

A few traditional shirt and suit-makers give vouchers to many large firms so their employees can claim discounts. It's, therefore, worth asking any friends you have that work in the city, to see if they have any unwanted vouchers, or check the internet before you go shopping, so that you can take advantage of the discount too. Like the bartering tip, if you've not found any discounts online, or through friends, it is sometimes just worth asking at the store itself.

Always Try Things On

Do ensure that you try things on before you buy them. It baffles me how many people don't do this, then wonder why things look slightly wrong on them. Sizes can vary from store to store and subtle differences in tailoring can make a big difference when you actually wear things. Taking a few extra minutes to try something on can mean the difference between looking a million dollars and not quite carrying something off.

Go Bespoke

If you can afford to have tailor-made clothes or feel like splashing out as a one off, do it! You don't have to pay Saville Row prices if you shop around a bit. Many online retailers offer cheap tailoring if you send them your measurements and a picture of what you want made. Ebay is particularly good for this. You'll be faced with plenty of options if you use the words 'custom made' in your search options, but do remember to always check a person's feedback.

Cheap tailoring is also widely available if you travel to the Far East, India, or even some of the Mediterranean countries; check travel guides or ask hotels for local recommendations. Tailoring is especially popular with tourists in the Far East and many local shops and hotels will be only too happy to point you in the right direction. Many of these tailors will keep your measurements on file so that you can order items at a later date from your home country. Some of these tailors make regular marketing trips to Europe and America; so do check the internet or corporate magazines for these.

Buy Clothing from a High Street Store and Get Them Adjusted at Your Local Tailor

This is a happy medium between getting something tailor-made and not spending a fortune on doing so. Buying things from the high street sometimes means sacrificing what could be a perfect fit. By taking an item of clothing to a local tailor for adjustments, you can give your high street outfit the look of a bespoke piece by putting in a few extra darts and by making sure it fits perfectly. It will cost you a lot less too.

Customise

This can be one way of individualising an outfit that you buy from a shop. Your local haberdashery department is a gold mine of ideas for revamping old clothes or even making new ones more exciting. Something as simple as sewing on a more interesting hemline can make an outfit look more expensive than it really was in the first place. If you feel uncomfortable about doing this yourself, you can buy iron-on beads, fabrics, hemlines or of course you can take the ideas to your local tailor to do it for you.

Designer Outlet Centres

Designer outlet centres tend to be out of the main city centres, but are often worth the trip for the sheer amount of money saving ideas that they offer. They are an especially good idea if you're looking to revamp your wardrobe. You're likely to be able to pick up more unusual things, at a fraction of the price.

Go Vintage

This is another great way to pick up something original and different. Clothes from vintage stores will often be true one-of-a-kind items. Some vintage shops offer outfits for very reasonable prices and will ensure that you have something that no one else is likely to own, so will help you to stand out from the crowd.

Use the Internet

I am a big fan of this method of shopping for clothes. It is important for you to know your exact measurements rather than simply relying on your dress size though, as different sites may have subtle variations on the standard sizes. If you find an outfit you like, email the site and ask for the exact measurements of the item you want. By using this method, you're much more likely to get a perfect fit and you can shop for more unusual items or items from foreign countries. This can be helpful when you have a good idea of what you're looking for, or if you're simply looking for something a little bit different.

Get some assistance

If you feel like you'd like a little extra help in this department, have a think about people whose style you like and admire. Well-dressed people tend to have at least a small passion for clothes and would probably be delighted to help you. You can of course also come and see me at www.howtobecaptivating.com if you want me to help you create your own before and after transformation. I have personally worked with and created all the transformations that you see in this book and I'd be delighted to help you create your signature look, brand and help you develop your very own captivating presence.

Whoever you use for help, use the time to get some new ideas. Even if you can't afford all of the suggestions, you can use what is said and find similar styles of garment on the internet, other shops or even in the depths of your existing wardrobe. For example, if you had never tried pinstripe suits before, but decide after your consultation that pinstripes are a really good look for you, then you will find a multitude of shops which will stock different types of pinstripe garments; it's as easy as that.

Chapter Summary

- Think about what the happiest, most successful, best version of you would want to wear – then wear it!
- Dress for your business personality.
- Don't be afraid to shop around or bargain for exactly what you want.
- Always try things on.

Chapter 7

"I want to feel like *me!*"
Dressing for Your Personality with The Style Dial

Create your own visual style... let it be unique for yourself and yet identifiable for others.
Orson Welles

Dressing for your personality is one of the secrets of appearing completely authentic from that first moment that someone meets you. Each person has their own individual style, all of which can look incredible in its own way, but put a person in the wrong style for their personality, and it can lead to lack of trust in the people that we are trying to attract. For example, think about The Queen dressing in a yellow tracksuit? Or Madonna deciding that she wanted to dress like Margaret Thatcher? Perhaps a glam rock star, like Marc Bolan (T-Rex) in a black suit? Somehow these just *feel* wrong, don't they? Although these seem like extreme examples, their personalities are reflected, to a large extent, in their personal style. In fact, style is a big part of how we perceive people and their personalities; it gives us our very first insight into who they are. Dressing in a way that is in keeping with who you are will let people focus on the message that you're projecting, rather than subconsciously thinking that there is something amiss with your appearance. Of course there are many different types of people and many different ways that people can look amazing. To give you a helping hand, if you really don't have a clue, I have created a Style Dial, originally inspired by my good friend and branding expert, Izzy Gainford.

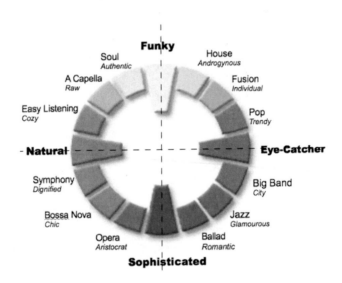

Of course, your style may change depending on the environment that you're in, but at your core, you will fall into one of these 12 styles, although you may have hints of some others. You will also see the style group that is the direct opposite of yours; this is a style that you should really avoid – unless absolutely necessary – as it is the one that will look the most incongruent on you, but as a personality, it is potentially the one that you will most learn from as they are your complete opposite. You will also find in some ways a more 'evolved' version of the style that comes up just before yours, so you will have a lot to learn from the types either side of you too.

Read through the descriptions to find out which personality type feels the most like you. Of course, there are not just 12 types of people in the world. We are all individuals and will have our own slant on these styles. However, these groupings are designed to give you a place to start defining your style so that it is in keeping with your personality. Once you've read through the styles and settled on which group you belong to, look at the style tips associated with that group and use them for reference next time you have to choose something to wear, or something to buy.

THE FUNKY GROUP

The Funky Group is the direct opposite of The Sophisticated Group. This group is modern and creative, very unlikely to conform to societal norms. They will act and dress in a way that pleases them, and will probably not care one bit about what anyone else thinks! They are either likely to ooze complete confidence, or be so creative, that their creativity far outweighs any shyness that they might feel.

HOUSE

Androgynous
Witty – Intellectual - Inclusive

House Personality

Like House music, House people are very inclusive, energetic, and not afraid to be different. House exudes a quiet confidence rather than a brashness and is comfortable in his or her own skin. There is a gentle wittiness to House, with an intellectual edge.

You're likely to get a lot of interesting conversations on a variety of topics, but they do not indulge in personal gossip or share too much about themselves. You'll find them absolutely fascinating, but try and get *too* close, and you'll end up feeling that they are a bit of an enigma. You may feel like House is hiding something from you, but in fact they are probably hiding even from themselves! They tend to focus on things in life that stimulate them and make them happy, but may risk burying more difficult issues deep within.

There is a real inclusiveness about House; despite potentially having deep secrets, House does not discriminate and welcomes everyone that comes their way regardless of their age, colour, walk of life or whatever else! Overall, House is upbeat, interesting, and may come across as slightly aloof, but you'll be delighted to have them in your life!

House Style

House is not afraid to cross over into styles of the opposite sex. You may see House ladies in ties, or House men in eyeliner! Overall, the look is likely to be smart, fashionable and creative, but neutralised as far as possible, so that their masculinity or femininity is not immediately obvious from their clothes.

House Women like: Straight cut clothes, blazers, their boyfriend's wardrobe!

House Men like: Skinny jeans or trousers, make up, slim fitted shirts or t-shirts.

Icons: Twiggy, Keira Knightly, David Bowie.

FUSION

Individual
Independent – Self-Assured – Feisty

Fusion Personality

Like Fusion music, Fusion people like to throw the rule book out and create something from scratch that is individualistic, and perfectly suited to what was intended. Fusions know what they want, know how to get it and haven't followed any of society's norms to get there. They are so confident in their own skin that many look up to them, and no matter what they look like, the sheer confidence that they exude makes it hard not to find them attractive. Fusion spends little to no time worrying what others think of them. They are also fiercely protective of the people around them – if you have a Fusion friend, you certainly have a protector for life. You certainly do not want to be on the wrong side of them though – only Big Band is capable of being a match for Fusion, if you do manage to upset them!

Fusions can be the centre of attention, but only because they are so distinctive in their personality, you can't help but notice them. It is definitely not something that they are consciously going out and seeking.

Fusion Style

Fusion would be absolutely disgusted that we're putting them into a style category! The style is creative, but in an utterly individual way. There isn't anyone on this planet that's going to look quite like Fusion, although many will try and copy their style. They are leaders, trendsetters, and they do sometimes get it wrong, but you will always have fun looking at them.

Fusion likes: Contrasting styles and colours, anything eclectic and bold that no one else could quite pull off.

Icons: Madonna, Sarah Jessica Parker, Jean Paul Gaultier.

POP

Trendy
Young – Fun – Carefree

Pop Personality

Pop is the youngest of all the personality styles, coming across as fusion's teenage child! The confidence is carefree rather than feisty. Pop people will try anything once and and just like Pop music, they will always be evolving and willing to try new things. Pop will be highly likely to be in an usual job – you know the one we all dreamt of as children, but didn't think that anyone *actually* did. That's because the Pops of this world will have taken those roles!

Like the other members of the funky family, Pop can come across as aloof at times, but only because they inhabit their own world, rather than it being a deliberate act. Their childlike charm, however, helps to create some strong friendships and an abundance of people who would drop everything just to be around them.

Pop Style

Pop doesn't dress for other people, but absolutely thrives on the style compliments that they get. They won't be afraid of boho and ethnic styles, if they happen to be in fashion right now. Pop will want the latest catwalk creation, well before it hits the high street! Unlike Fusion, the inspiration for style comes from the style magazines and icons, rather than the style being created entirely from within. Pop will *always* be on trend, and amongst their pier groups, probably leading it!

Pop likes: Whatever's been on the runway today.

Icons: Kate Moss, Sienna Miller, David Beckham.

THE EYE-CATCHER GROUP

Eye-Catchers are the direct opposite of The Natural Group. This group were born to be noticed, both in their style and personality. Like The Funky Group, they are creative, and to the outside world do ooze complete confidence, but this is tempered by a real desire to be liked and accepted by the people around them.

BIG BAND

City

Striking – Honest – Independent

Big Band Personality

Big Band music and people can't fail to be noticed as they are kitted out with the best of everything in order to make a striking and overall BIG impression. Big Band people are independent, strong and like all the eye-catchers, love attention. Their attention loving personality often makes them the life and soul of the party. Big band is also painfully honest – to the point of being offensive at times, but this directness also makes them thoroughly endearing. You also know that if you have a Big Band in your life, you better brace yourself for some home truths (all meant with love of course!)

Big Band comes across as being immensely confident, but is a real teddy bear underneath that bold facade. If you're not scared to get to know them in the first place (let's face it, you may be a little apprehensive approaching someone so outwardly confident), you'll find that they are completely loveable with a heart of gold, even if they do offend you at times.

Big Band Style

Just like their personality, Big Band lives to be noticed. This is style at its most dramatic and will probably turn quite a lot of heads. Like Fusion, this is not for those that want to hide in the corner of a room. They walk in, and you will notice. They always carry off their dramatic style with a level of sophistication that is sometimes not present in the funky style. The overall style will exude class, but may contain one or two accessories that break away from the norm, making this style very different to the Symphony's timeless elegance.

Big Band likes: Quality suits with a twist, designer fashions,

73

contrasting colours tastefully put together.
Icons: Elizabeth Hurley, Jane Fonda, Al Pacino.

JAZZ

Glamorous
Charming – Popular – Achiever

Jazz Personality

Both Jazz Music and Jazz people are experimental, infectious, and can't help attracting the crowds. They are not too fond of rules and convention, and often like to throw the rule book out to create something even better. Jazz is also like one of the popular kids at school. If she's a woman, girls want to be her, boys want to go out with her, and of course vice-versa for the men! Jazz is often the pack leader and takes a select few friends into the fold. Jazz can appear intimidating at times because so many people demand their attention and admire then, but once you have it, Jazz knows how to ooze charm. Jazz has a tendency to have an underlying need for love and attention. This is one of the reasons that they always strive for the best and ooze glamour in order to get the attention (and acceptance!) that they crave.

Like Big Band, once you get underneath the charismatic front, you will find a marshmallow core. Jazz people probably frequently upset people that haven't got their attention; they are at times in their own world and not overly perceptive. However, they'd be devastated to learn that someone had been hurt by their actions. Their vulnerability is not seen by many, but does run very deep and makes them even more endearing to those that know them.

Jazz Type

Flamboyance and ostentation are the order of the day, all tastefully put together to create pure glamour. Think Red Carpet fashion and glitz of any sort. Jazz also oozes quality. There will be nothing out of place – this look is put together absolutely perfectly with great attention to detail.

Jazz Women like: Sparkly accessories, anything uber feminine with a twist, quality custom designs.

Jazz Men like: Quality accessories, uber masculine clothing, quality custom designs, designer suits.

Icons: Paris Hilton, Goldie Hawn, Jude Law.

BALLAD

Romantic
Feminine – Sensitive – Trusting

Ballad Personality

Like Ballad music, Ballad people are incredibly romantic and not afraid to express their emotions and sensitivities with an endearing innocence. In fact, Ballad would be right at home in any fairy tale. Ballad women play the damsel in distress beautifully. Men (and other slightly more masculine women) will flock to her assistance – whatever she needs. In contrast, Ballad men will ooze romance, and make it his life's purpose to ensure that he and his woman live happily ever after!

Ballads are very trusting and sweet, but know how to work their charm to get what they want. The difference between them and Jazz is that the Ballads don't even know that it's called charm – it all comes so naturally! Ballads may be a little naïve about the big bad world, but as they'll be surrounded by people who'll want to look after them, what's the big deal really?

Ballad Style

Both Ballad men and women are going to have a sense of femininity and romance to their look. Luxury fabrics that are beautiful to touch are going to be the order of the day. If the fabrics are patterned, they will be gentle on the eye. As with Jazz,

Ballad pays great attention to detail. Want to make them really happy? Invite them to a black tie event; they will genuinely either be the belle of the ball or Prince Charming!

> Ballad likes: Frills and ruffles, velvet and silk, hearts and flowers, impeccable accessories.
> Icons: Marilyn Monroe, Doris Day, Prince Charming.

THE SOPHISTICATED GROUP

The Sophisticated Group is the direct opposite of The Funky Group. They have a love of the traditional and love the tried and tested classics when it comes to style. They are likely to do things that are in keeping with their character, and like The Eye-Catcher Group, really do care what people think about them. The Sophisticated Group really ooze dignity and class and will usually keep up appearances.

OPERA

Aristocrat
Charming – Opulent – Vulnerable

Opera Personality

Opera women let their femininity shine at every opportunity. And Opera men? Well, they just happen to be really good at connecting with women, whilst still maintaining their sense of masculinity.

Like Opera music, Opera people do favour a sense of the luxury associated with high society. They do feel the need to conform to societal norms, rather than being complete creatives, but unlike Symphony, they will let their luxuriant personalities shine through. Operas do feel a need to live up to what is expected of them, and have a need to be accepted by others. As with Jazz, not being accepted can be one of the things that will hurt Opera the most, but they go for a more conventional route to gain the approval. Whereas Jazz is not afraid of being a little off the wall at times, Opera will stick to the good old-fashioned wisdom!

Opera Style

Opera is conventional, with a hint of glamour. Like Jazz, they would be at home on the Red Carpet. Unlike Jazz, Opera would be much more likely to favour a conventional outfit, but dress it up with something luxurious and unexpected, giving the impression of sophistication, together with a few hints that they love sheer opulence and indulgence. They know that they need to be taken seriously, but will push the boundaries just a little bit to ensure that they keep a sense of their own individuality in their otherwise timeless styles.

> Opera likes: Elaborate accessories, quality fabrics, original pieces in classic styles.
> Icons: Victoria Beckham, Charlotte Goldenblatt nee York (Sex and the City), Prince Harry.

BOSSA NOVA

Chic
Socialite – Classy – Pretentious

Bossa Nova Personality

Bossa Novas are well travelled and know themselves and the world around them very well. These are the people to ask if you want contacts in certain places as they probably know them all – on a superficial level at least!

As with Bossa Nova music, Bossa Nova people are very sophisticated and never fail to create an impression that is simply chic. They won't stand out because she wants to shock – they really don't need to resort to such tactics as they already know that they're a million dollars! They are immensely comfortable in their own skin and only out to impress themselves. They are likely to hang out with people exactly like themselves, but there are those in wider society that can't help but be impressed by Bossa Nova's inner confidence. Certain elements, however, remain a mystery to all, except the cherished few that know them best.

Bossa Nova Style

Bossa Nova goes for high-end designer items that ooze sophistication. They would probably feel right at home in all the European fashion capitals, choosing the classic rather than the outrageous styles. They are very self-assured about their own style, and will probably be admired by many for their timeless fashion sense.

Bossa Nova likes: Impeccable tailoring, luxury fabrics, expensive jewellery and accessories.

Icons: Audrey Hepburn, Coco Chanel, James Bond.

SYMPHONY

Distinguished
Responsible – Regal – Reserved

Symphony Personality

Like Symphony music, Symphony people have a real sense of tradition and exude grandeur without even trying to. They are likely to be classically beautiful or handsome, with a real sense of what they want in the long term rather than someone who plays the "short term fun" game. Symphony people may actually put up with things that they don't necessarily like or enjoy in the short term if they feel that it will be for the greater good and will benefit themselves and others in the long term.

Symphonies are loyal, devoted, patient and strong. They can be a bit reserved, and may even feel a bit shy around the opposite sex. Underneath all that, you'll probably uncover a person who is very caring and will open up to you. (if you get to know them VERY well!)

Symphony Style

Think Royal Family. This style simply exudes pure class, but in an understated way. Classics are looking for quality, respectability and dare I say it – modesty! They are well groomed with not a hair out of place. They are also willing to spare no expense in order to get their style just right. Stepping outside what is expected, and probably revered by many, just would not be an option. They know that their style exudes quality and class and they do not need the drama of the eye-catchers to give out that message.

Symphony likes: Quality tailoring, traditional designs, classic tweed, simple pearls.

Icons: Lady Diana, Kate Middleton, Prince William.

THE NATURAL GROUP

The Natural Group is the direct opposite of the Eye-Catcher group. This group doesn't necessarily mind what the outside world thinks of their style, letting their warm, engaging, earthy and wise personality shine through instead.

Easy Listening
Cosy
Nurturing – Tolerant – Peaceful

Easy Listening Personality Type

Easy Listening is like Mother Earth. She is nurturing, caring and a joy to come home to.

They make environments cosy, they make you feel special with their quiet warmth, and their peacefulness automatically makes you forget why you ever bothered with the hustle and bustle of life. They are completely at home in nature, and very comfortable in their own lives. Like Easy Listening music, Easy Listening people make you feel like you're receiving a warm hug, just when you need it.

Easy Listening is very tolerant of people and situations, and is likely to avoid conflict at all costs. As their lifestyles are very comfortable, they are also likely to resist change, favouring the familiar rather than the unknown.

Easy Listening trusts the process of life and trusts that things will be just fine in the end. This attitude often ensures that they'll land on her feet and be just fine, despite not being as ambitious as the other personality types. This is the classic boy or girl next door that you just can't resist.

Easy Listening Style

Easy Listening people feel most like themselves when they feel comfortable. Easy Listening ladies probably prefer their riding boots to their heels and Easy Listening men really dislike wearing a suit to work. They love natural fibres, probably made in an ethical way. Neither sex are particularly bothered about accessories, unless they are going to add to the comfort that they want to feel. A little subtle tailoring, and focusing on a few key quality pieces can really help Easy Listening people to look effortlessly stylish.

Easy Listening loves: Natural materials, comfortable clothes, minimal accessories.
Icons: Sandra Bullock, Martha Stewart, Robert Pattinson.

A CAPELLA

Raw
Adventurous – Enthusiastic – Playful

A Capella Personality

A Capella can come across like the big child. Full of energy, health and vitality, this is a personality that sees everything in life as a game, which A Capella fully intends to enjoy to the max! There is nothing false about them – like A Capella Music, the personality is very raw, very real, and very infectious. A Capellas have the spirit of travel and adventure, and are out to explore everything that the world can offer! They are a lot of fun to be around and definitely like to emphasise the "life" in the work/life balance equation. Often they will end up having a career that they adore – after all, why do something if you don't love it?

A Capella is very open and has an enthusiasm for anything new and exciting. They are constantly striving to learn more and improve themselves, but as a result can get bored easily and find it difficult to take responsibility.

A Capella Style

As the name suggests, A Capella is a style that needs no adornment. It's likely that their looks are naturally rosy and healthy-looking. They are, therefore, the least style conscious people in the Style Dial, but nevertheless still manage to look amazing. They will most likely favour sporty casual looks, allowing them to do anything adventurous at a moments notice.

A Capella loves: Anything that allows them to move easily, fun colours.

Icons: Mel C, Charlie Dimmock, Steve Irwin.

SOUL

Authentic
Strong – Nurturing – Wise

Soul Personality

Soul is a role model and a peacemaker. Like Soul music, Soul

People have a real depth to them, and share the wisdom of their experiences. They have strong family values and are admired by many because of their wisdom, maturity and ability to remain neutral and heal rifts. Soul strives for the dream family life, gaining the most happiness from complete comfort and serenity in their personal circumstances.

As Soul often does things for the greater good, there is a bit of a self-sacrificing nature to their personality, and it is very important that they do not forget what their own needs are. Overall, they are very caring people, and in return will attract people who care about them very deeply. They will also inspire many by their serene example.

Soul Style

As with soul music, because Soul has so much depth and raw talent, they don't usually feel the need be too showy in their fashion sense. They will choose items that are incredibly tasteful, but they are not looking to be the centre of attention (at least not

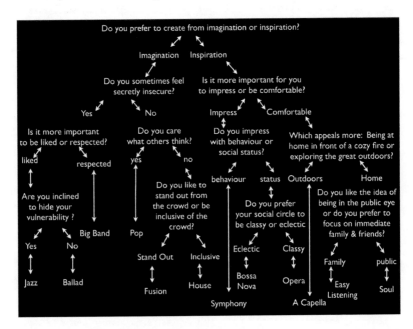

with their clothes!). It is more likely that they will want people to notice the message, not the clothes, and simple elegance of the styles they do choose to match the peacefulness of their nature.

Soul loves: Neutral colours, natural fabrics, simple cuts, understated accessories.

Icons: Oprah Winfrey, Barack and Michelle Obama.

If you have read through all the descriptions and are still confused as to which of them resonates the most with you, I have prepared a short quiz for you to find out which style is the most likely to be you. Of course to me, style, like personality, is an intuitive exploration and much like the zodiac, where a star sign won't tell you *everything* about a person, the style dial only acts as your guide rather than your bible.

Chapter Summary

- Dress for your personality. This will add to your overall congruence in front of clients.
- The style categories can be represented in the Style Dial.
- The style dial is not a replacement for your intuitive sense of self and style. It is a starting point on your journey to dressing for your personality.

Chapter 8

"I'm bored of my black suit!"
The Psychology of Colour

"Mere colour, unspoiled by meaning, and unailled with definite form, can speak to the soul in a thousand different ways."
Oscar Wilde

So why do most lawyers dress in black? Why does London Underground staff have an orange uniform? And why do

McDonalds, KFC and Burger King all have the same colour scheme? It's no accident – apparently these colours encourage their diners to eat and leave quickly. Now think about a fine Italian restaurant using fast food colours? It just doesn't feel right, does it?

A well-tailored black suit may send out a message that you work in the city as an accountant. Change the same suit to shocking pink, and suddenly you may be giving out the impression that you work for a hip TV channel.

Like it or not, the colours that you're wearing on yourself, and using in your business, are sending out a subconscious message to everyone that you come in contact with. If you haven't thought about the right colours to use in your business, you could be turning off your target market without even realising why. This is why you should be giving colour at least a little consideration prior to meeting people, and certainly prior to promoting your business.

There are four factors to consider in relation to a particular colour:

1. Hue: The colour itself
2. Temperature: Cool, warm or neutral
3. Value: Light Dark or Medium
4. Intensity: Whether it appears clear or muted

Any person can wear any colour, but the other three factors will determine whether it suits you and your personality. Think for example about the colour blue. A royal blue will probably be classified to be cool, medium and clear, giving out a very direct, powerful message. Compare this to a powder blue, which will more than likely be cool, light and muted. In comparison, this blue would give off a much softer message than its royal relative.

Have a look at the picture below. This is Jules who runs a company called *Feel Glorious*. The outfit on the left is in a gentle

powder blue, which does not reflect the vibrancy of her brand, or her business, at all. On the right, is a picture of Jules after our time together. Here we have put her in a bright red dress, which matches the vibrancy of her brand. A brand that is dedicated to people feeling healthy and, of course, glorious! In fact, she has since bought the same dress in a vibrant teal blue. It wasn't the fact that blue was the wrong colour for her to wear, but in the wrong tone, it was a disaster for her business image.

So where do you start when it comes to figuring out the right colours for your business? Both your colouring, and your personality, will be important in this determination. I like to compare each of the groupings to the elements, to give you some idea as to their personality as well as the actual colour.

Fire

Fire people are generally dark haired with deep eyes, although a few white blonde haired people also fall into this category. The skin tones tend to be clear with blue or pink undertones, and as a result, Fire can carry very rich colours, closest to the primary colours.

Colours: Warm and clear
Personality: Bold, no nonsense, individual

Water

Water people are often natural blondes or brunettes with pale eyes. Their complexions, like winter, have blue or pink undertones.

Colours: Cool and muted
Personality: Gentle, reserved, classy

Earth

Earth complexions have golden undertones to their skin and eyes. Many redheads, and dark haired people with golden brown eyes fall into the Earth category.

Colours: Warm and muted
Personality: Deep, warm, passionate

Air

Air people also have golden undertones, but tend to have more creamy, white or peach skin tones. They may have strawberry blonde hair, rosy cheeks and freckles with blue or green eyes. Their colours will be cool and clear.

Colours: Cool and clear
Personality: Fun, vibrant, carefree

Ether

Ether people conjure up the image of flawlessness. They are conventionally attractive, and have an almost spiritual air about them. Rather than being a conventional 'type', ether colouring should be used to suit those in industries with a therapeutic or healing slant.

Colours: Light and clear, with a natural or colourless slant
Personality: Spiritual, ethereal, wise

The best way to test which colours are going to be best for you is to hold up a variety of colours to your face and see which 'group' suits you best. Please also consider your personality (or the personality that you most want conveyed!) when choosing your preferred colour group. As you hold each colour up to your skin, pay particular attention to what the colour does to your hair, eyes and skin tone. Do they bring your eyes to life? Do they make you look washed out? You should very soon get a sense of which colours accentuate your features and your personality the most. Some colours will make your skin look warmer and others will accentuate negative features. By taking some time to compare different colours and how they look against your skin, you'll have an idea of what to purchase in the future and what colours will suit you best. You don't have to ban any colours from your wardrobe – changing the tone of a colour will usually be

Red	Excitement, Speed, Danger, Energy, Strength, Sex
Blue	Authority, Trust, Reliability, Coolness, Trust, Reliability
Yellow	Sunshine, Creativity, Warmth, Happiness, Optimism
Orange	Playfulness, Warmth, Vibrant, Passion
Green	Growth, Abundance, Money, Harmony, Balance, Health
Purple	Royalty, Spirituality, Wisdom, Dignity, Sophistication
Pink	Romance, Gentleness, Femininity, Sweet, Nurture
White	Pure, Virginal, Clean, Neutral
Black	Elegant, Seductive, Mystery, Stability, Strength, Solemnity
Gold	Prestige, Elite, Expensive Expensive
Silver	Prestige, Cold, Scientific
Gray	Middle of the road
Brown	Reliability, Stability, Grounded-ness

enough to make sure that it suits you perfectly. For example, if mustard is not quite your colour, but you love yellow, you could try a sunshine-yellow instead.

The other part of determining which colours you should be using is to consider what your ideal client, or person you want to attract, will be most drawn to. Although the tone of the colour will usually be dependent on the way that you look, the colour itself can be determined by your mood, your personality and what you most want to attract, in the moment that you use it.

I have provided the table below as a rough guide as to what each colour means to get you started on your colour journey.

Chapter Summary

- Different colours will send out different subliminal messages to the people that you come across.
- Figure out which colour group suits you best; not only in terms of your looks but also in terms of your personality.
- Use colour in accordance with the message that you want to evoke.

Chapter 9

"How can I make gorgeous clothes look good on me?"
The Finishing Touches

"I don't understand how a woman can leave the house without fixing herself up a little – if only out of politeness. And then, you never know, maybe that's the day she has a date with destiny. And it's best to be as pretty as possible for destiny."
Coco Chanel

It's true. You don't have to spend a lot of money on new clothes to look good. Sometimes, it's best to work with your existing wardrobe – you can genuinely find a lot of gems amongst what you already have. They may only need a minor revamp to bring them up to date and just in line with the presence that you want to create. The key is to look at what you have with new eyes, applying all the techniques that you have learnt in this book so far. Do the colours suit your business? Do the styles really match your personality? What is your look really saying to people?

The secret the worlds' most stylish people have mastered is the art of accessorising. Get this right, and you can make 'boring' look sensational, 'high street' look designer, and 'sloppy-casual' look chic. Once you've mastered the skill, you'll always look great whatever you wear, and the best part is that you can find incredible accessories at any budget, so it's a great way to stretch your wardrobe and save money.

Kim's Story

Kim had not been shopping for a long time, and like many of my other clients, specifically did not want to spend any more on updating her wardrobe. Instead, she wanted to go through what she already owned, largely from the 1980s, in order to exude the right image to attract corporate clients. Although a lot of Kim's 1980s suits were outdated, by teaming up the skirts with her existing feminine blouses, some belts that she would have never dreamed of using with smart clothing and the right shoes, she was able to convey a very modern look just by using her existing wardrobe. She was even able to use her trademark necklace for special occasions!

If you're dressing for your business, depending on your industry, it can be useful to have one accessory that becomes your 'trademark' piece. This is an item that adds intrigue to your outfit, or lets people associate that item with you.

If you're unable to revamp your style with what you already have, often, all that's needed is to team things up with something that you wouldn't have expected, and perhaps to splash out on a few well thought out accessories.

As with clothes and colour, my starting point with accessories is to recognise that they are an extension and expression of who you are. For example, do you feel like you're a bold personality? A striking piece of costume jewellery may be just what you need. Are you sophisticatedly conservative? Perhaps some simple, good quality gold jewellery would be more suited to you. Are you uber feminine? Perhaps infusing some gentle florals into your look would be just what you need. Whatever way you choose to go, accessories can say so much! Here are some great ideas to get you started.

Jewellery

All that is needed to take a lovely outfit to something absolutely outstanding, is a striking piece of jewellery. For special events, you can use your bolder pieces of jewellery, but it is also nice to have a few signature pieces of jewellery to wear every day.

Shay's Story

In this picture, you will see the jewellery I wear everyday; a mystic topaz ring given to me by my mum. A citrine ring which I wear to remind me of my nan's favourite colour and as a symbol of abundance. A prayer bead bracelet – a reminder that God is looking after me, and a silver band with the inscription 'Imagine, Create, Become' which is a message that I always want to remember. Although I have many other different pieces of jewellery, I love using these pieces as everyday wear as they all mean something specific to me, making them my signature pieces.

The More Basic the Outfit, the Bolder Your Accessories Can Be

The difference between an amazing outfit, and one that has gone too far, is the balance between the actual outfit and the accessories. If you're already wearing something that is very bold in colour or style, your accessories need to be lower key. For example, a polka dot dress will generally not need bold costume jewellery teamed up with it, as the pattern will already be making a strong impact. In contrast, if you're wearing a simple shift dress, a bold cocktail ring or an amazing pair of shoes will be able to take the dress from day to night easily.

The Use of Colour

Adding a sparkle of colour to an otherwise plain outfit can also work brilliantly, but as a general rule, try and keep your accessories in the same colour family as the rest of your outfit. E.g. if your outfit is black (a fire colour), bold red accessories will work far better than a muted blue from the elegant colour family.

Don't Wear Too Many Accessories at Once

Remember when you were 5 years old and liked to play in mummy's closet and with her make up collection? Well, if you go over the top, it'll probably resemble your childhood days. There really can be too much of a good thing, so don't wear too many accessories that make a statement. For example, you don't need to team up your statement earrings with a statement necklace and a multitude of cocktail rings – although they may look nice individually, using them all is going to be a disaster. One or two main pieces are more than enough.

Belts

Belts are fantastic to either fake or accentuate an hour-glass figure. They can also be extremely useful in adding a subtle dash of colour or glamour to an otherwise boring outfit. A few of my favourites are:

Skinny Belts

These work particularly well with a fitted dress or jumpsuit to add a subtle dash of colour or emphasis to your waist. Some skinny belts go around twice, which in a lot of cases can look even better. Try bright colours, animal patterns or metallics for the best effects.

Medium Belts

My personal view is that belts are more interesting when they are slightly wider or slightly skinnier than normal. It takes your look from "normal" to 'special'. However, there is a place for medium belts, particularly if they are made with good materials or have an interesting buckle feature. They can work well with jeans to give them a more formal look if you're wearing jeans with a blouse or anything with pre-sewn belt loops.

Large Belts

Other than under-bust corsets, large belts are the best at defining your waist and cinching in oversized outfits. They can look lovely over outfits that are not otherwise tailored.

Under-bust Corsets

For those of you that are brave enough, these are my absolute favourite accessory. There is no better accessory for cinching in the waist, and they always add a touch of instant glamour and femininity. If you aren't sure what they are, you'll see one of mine in the picture overleaf. The well made ones can be a bit expensive, but if you can afford it and fancy the style, you won't regret investing in a steel boned corset as this will always retain its shape and last you far longer than their cheaper equivalents.

The Right Shoes

A great outfit should always be completed with the right pair of shoes! However, as much as I love skyscraper heels, they are not always necessary to make you look like a million dollars. These would be my recommendations for shoes that every girl should have, if you don't already have a great shoe collection!

A Fun Pair of Flats

Every girl needs something that she can run around town in. I know that Carrie Bradshaw does everything in Manolos, but living in the real world can be a bit hard on your feet, so why not make things a little easier on yourself? By making them fun, you can still feel good about the way that you look.

Classic Heels

There are so many different types of heels around; you'd do well to go with something just to match your current wardrobe and personality. As a basic show wardrobe, I'd recommend heels in a basic black (or other appropriate work colour) and one pair in a fun colour such as red. As a third pair, I would also recommend getting one pair of nude heels, as these will lengthen your legs as well as being versatile enough to go with most outfits.

If you're not a fan of really high heels because of the comfort factor, I would definitely recommend something with a concealed platform, like the shoes pictured below. As these already have a ½ inch platform in the front, the heel is deceptively high. Therefore, you can give the illusion of height whilst maintaining your own comfort.

Evening Shoes

As well as your collection of heels, it would also be great to have at least one pair of good evening shoes. These obviously come in a large variety of styles and colours, but if you're limited to just one, I would go with something strappy in either gold, silver or nude so that you can team them up with most evening outfits that you're likely to wear.

Chic Boots

If you live in Fiji, Hawaii or the Cayman Islands, you can probably ignore this tip. For the rest of us, I have personally found it very useful to have some boots handy to wear with my suits and other outfits. If you're only getting one pair, I recommend that you go for something in a neutral colour so that it will go with most of your outfits, in a smart style such as riding boots, although of course many of you won't need much convincing to go shopping for more!

Scarves

These are not just for keeping you warm in the winter! Those of the non-wool variety can also be useful for adding a dash of interest or colour to even the dullest of outfits. Patterned scarves can go with plain outfits, and some experimental ways of putting them on can create a look that is truly unique. Don't be afraid to be creative; as well as simply tying them around your neck, you may be able to use certain scarves as a wrap, a belt or even a top. You can also use them with a broach or belt buckle to create even more styles.

Hair and Make Up

Sometimes it's the little things that help the most. Perhaps all you need is a subtle revamp with your haircut or make-up to help you let go of your old inhibitions and show the world the new you. In one case, I knew a beautiful brunette woman with long hair who decided to add blonde highlights and go for a cropped haircut. Obviously, this was a drastic step, but the change looked incredible and helped her to feel incredible. The changes you make need not be as drastic as that, but having a consultation with your local hairdresser or the make-up counters at department stores may contribute to you feeling like a new, fabulous version of you. Sometimes you won't believe the difference that a few subtle changes can make once you ask for advice. Most make-up counters will give you this information free of charge or offer to do make-overs for very low prices which are in any event refundable against purchases. Similarly, most hairdressers will do a style consultation free of charge.

Making it Easy

Most of you will already have quite a few accessories, so it may not be necessary to go out shopping for more. However, it is very useful to sort them out into themes, metal types and colour families within your own wardrobe, so that when it comes to completing your outfit, you always have a collection of accessories ready to go with it. You can also take photographs of each grouping to remind you of what you have when you come to accessorise, as you may not be keeping your belts, handbags and jewellery in the same space. By sorting them out in this way, it will also help you to see what else you may need to complete your accessory wardrobe.

Chapter Summary

- Accessories are an easy and cost effective way to revamp your current wardrobe.
- Always use accessories that match your brand and personality.
- You can use one key piece as your "trademark" to make you immediately recognisable to your audience.
- The more basic your outfit, the bolder your accessories can be.
- A splash of colour with a bright accessory may be all that a plain outfit needs to give it a new lease of life.
- Don't wear too many accessories at once.

Chapter 10

"I don't know what it is about her..."
Scent – uality

"A woman's perfume tells more about her than her handwriting."
Christian Dior

Scents are one of the most popular subconscious signals we can use to trigger attraction. In fact, since caveman days, our brain has been trained to pick potential partners based purely on scent. A staggering 84% of people believe that perfume has the power to turn them on and off, and sometimes it makes no sense as to why. Fragrances can enhance someone's feelings and emotions, and can even change your perceptions of someone, so getting it right could just give you the little extra boost that you need in order to catch someone's attention. Your clients, friends and even dates, will notice with their subconscious (if not conscious) mind, and you may as well do everything you can to attract the right people to you! But remember, don't overdo it! Our body already emits natural odours designed to draw us to our perfect partners, so a gentle mist is often all you need to add to your natural scent.

What Are Perfumes?

A perfume is a mixture of essential oils, aroma compounds, fixatives, and solvents. These all work together in order to create the scent, and to make it last longer. All perfumes have a 'top note', which is the initial scent. This will last around 10 minutes, leaving behind the real heart of the scent. There is a 'middle note' which develops after the initial scent evaporates, designed to perfectly blend the 'top note' and 'base note'. The base note is the true scent. It works like a bouquet of flowers, perfectly blended together to create a unified scent. The 'base note' will be the scent that you're left with after a few hours of wearing it. This is why it is so important to find out what a perfume will smell like long after those initial minutes when you get sprayed by the shop assistant!

Due to the delicate composition of perfume, they interact differently according to your skin type. If you have dry skin, it's likely that you won't retain a perfume's top note for very long at all, whereas oily skin will retain the scents longer, meaning that you will be able to retain a much softer scent over time. A perfume will generally last about 3 years from the date it was bottled. Once you buy it, ensure that you take care of it by storing it out of direct sunlight. Just as the climate can affect the way that the perfume smells on you, its storage can impact its shelf life.

How to Choose a Perfume

When you go shopping for a perfume, there are a few different types that you can buy. These are the most common:

Eau de Parfume

This contains approximately 10-20% of aromatic compounds. They are the longest lasting of all the perfume types and typically available for men's perfumes, as scents generally last a little bit longer on ladies.

Eau de Toilette

This contains approximately 5-15% of aromatic compounds. They are not as strong as the other types of perfume, so won't typically last as long, but they are still extremely popular, and should see you through an evening easily. They are also less intense than the other types of perfume, but the subtly of them can work really well if you just want to give off a hint of a scent.

Perfume Extract

This is the most expensive type of perfume, as it is the most concentrated, typically containing 20% of aromatic compounds, but can contain as much as 40%. They are not as common as the other types of perfume, but if this is the one for you, know that you will only need a few drops in order to smell good all day!

If you don't have a favourite scent yet, it's worth experimenting in order to find one that suits you. Just because a certain scent smells good on your best friend doesn't mean that it is going to work for you. Our scent is unique, according to our very own body chemistry and pH balance. A perfume is designed to interact with your already natural scent, so the smell will vary according to our own individual chemistry. It is also not a good idea to buy perfumes when you're going through any hormonal changes, for example, pregnancy. This not only changes your natural body chemistry, but it can also subtly affect your sense of smell.

So head to your local perfume section and experiment with a few different scents to see which ones work for you the best.

Don't be shy in asking the sales person to help you, or to tell them about any perfumes that you do like, including any old favourites that you may already have at home. They will be able to direct you straight to other similar scents, or at the very least, perfumes that come from the same group. Each different perfume that you like, will give the salesperson clues as to the one that is really suited to you. Buying a perfume is an investment and expression of your personality. We all have many facets to us, and the more information that you're able to share, the more you'll be able to express about yourself through your scent. If you're able to, leave the scent on for a little while in order to see how it settles on your skin, as some will not last for more than a few hours and others will smell different after a while.

If you want to experiment with a few scents at the same time, it can be very difficult to remember what each scent smells like. The human nose can only cope with about 10 different perfume scents at any given time, unless you're a trained nose, and there are a very small number of those in the whole world! One way to counter this effect is to sniff coffee beans in between each scent, so that you do not get all the scents confused. Some perfume counters even have a jar of coffee available for you to clear the smell of many different scents (although obviously they do not put this on display). The coffee helps you to focus on new scents that you may want to try.

When you have decided on which perfume to purchase, remember to store it in a cool, and preferably dimly lit place. Once the bottle is opened, it will last for approximately 3 years if you look after it properly, so make sure that you store it well in order to lengthen its lifespan.

So let's get to the fun part – what kind of scent should *you* go for?

Well, perfumes come in 'families'. Everyone will naturally be drawn to certain families over others, and the people most attracted to us, will be likely to be drawn to those scents too. I'm sure you may have heard many people say that perfume purchasing is a very personal thing; you really do have to know someone well to be able to choose the right scent for them. For this reason, it's definitely not a good idea to buy a scent just because it's the latest thing or because your local store are having a sale. A perfume is a further investment into your personality and the scent will enhance the aura that is you. Choose wisely.

Green

Green scents include smells of freshly cut grass, leaves, and anything that reminds you of the great natural outdoors. They are often blended with woody, floral and herbal scents, for example, pine or juniper. These types of scent are suitable for both sexes, but as such, they do not work quite so well for bringing out that masculine or feminine allure that we all want sometimes! Where to use them: Daytime, anytime you're in the great outdoors.

Personality type: A Capella, House.

Examples: *Chanel No. 19, Ralph Lauren Safari, Escada Sport Country Weekend, Sung Alfred Sung, Escada Magnetism, Adidas Adrenaline Woman.*

Fresh

These scents are full of fruity, green and refreshing smells. Think of the smell of cut grass, dew, and lemon zest. Also in this category are the citrus scents, which give the wearer a very fresh, young and energising feel. Overall, fresh scents blend together to create a very crisp and clean result, for that utterly vibrant feel!

Where to use them: Daytime, the great outdoors or an evening out somewhere very young and funky!

Personality type: A Capella, Easy Listening, House, Pop.
Examples: *Clinique Happy, Burberry Weekend for Women, Cartier Eau de Cartier for Women, Jo Malone Grapefruit, Calvin Klein CK One, The Gap Close.*

Floral

Want to ooze femininity? Well, the florals are for you. These are the most popular types of scent for women and there is an abundance of them available. Obviously they include all types of flowers, but can often be mixed with a more woody or spicy scent to create an extra air of delicious complexity!

Where to use them: Anywhere where you feel you need to exude romance and femininity, especially when you're meeting the man in your life, his parents, or wanting to attract someone new!

Personality Type: Pure florals are suited to Ballad, Opera and Easy Listening, but Jazz, Bossa Nova and Symphony would probably really love the more complex fragrances in this range.

Examples: *Chanel No 5, Karl Lagerfeld Chloe, Lancome Tresor and Anna Sui, Beautiful (Estee Lauder), Happy to Be (Clinique), Summer (Kenzo) , Vera Wang (Vera Wang).*

Oriental

These are the scents that ooze class, but if we're comparing to the florals, we have here a scent that is sophisticated rather than girly and spells seduction rather than romance! One site even described oriental as the fragrance "equivalent of a cleavage and a killer pair of stilettos"! Think of the smell of vanilla, cinnamon and other "spices", blended with exotic flowers such as orchids and you have an oriental dream!

Where to use them: These are for glamorous events, or anywhere where you just want to add a touch of class. Perfect for that winter ball, Christmas parties, or for pure seduction. The choice is yours!

Personality Type: Symphony, Bossa Nova, Jazz, Big Band, Fusion.

Examples: *Elizabeth Taylor Black Pearls, Yves Saint Laurent Opuim, Guerlain Shalimar, Givenchy Organza, Yves Saint Laurent Opium, Versace Crystal Noir, Obsession (Calvin Klein) — Euphoria (Calvin Klein).*

Woody

This is not just about the tree in your back garden, these scents include some of the most beautiful smelling woods, such as sandalwood or cedar wood. They are often blended with a touch of spice, to add a little pizazz! They may have a base scent such as bark or moss, evoking the image of gardens or forests. These work particularly well as masculine scents, but there are plenty of woody scents for the ladies too!

Where to use them: These scents evoke the feeling of a romantic day out in the country, or that cosy home feel when you're out in the city. Use it to inspire the feeling of care and nurture with a tiny hint of adventure lurking beneath the surface! Personality Type: Soul, A Capella and Easy Listening would absolutely fall in love with these!

Examples: *Estee Lauder Knowing, Chanel No. 19, Britney Spears Believe, Ralph Lauren Romance, Gucci Envy Me.*

Spicy

Quite simply, these are the scents of sugar, spice and all things nice! Think of all those wonderful spices in your mum's kitchen cupboard, with notes of cinnamon, cardamom and cloves amongst many others – mmmmm. They are extremely alluring, but with a sense of underlying comfort which can be simply irresistible! They have a more mature edge and depth than some of the floral scents, so they can evoke an air of mystery rather than just being purely romantic.

Where to use them: romantic nights in or where you're in the mood to evoke the romantic night in feeling, with a touch of mystery!

Personality Type: Fusion, Big Band, Jazz, Bossa Nova, Easy Listening.

Examples: *Chanel Coco, Jo Malone Vetyver, BCBG Girls, Givenchy Ysatis, Estee Lauder Cinnabar.*

Oceanic

Oceanic is a very modern scent, pioneered only in 1991 by Christian Dior's *Dune*. They are synthetically created to evoke the ocean or mountain air. They evoke a similar mood to the fresh fragrances, without being so obviously "outdoorsy" or youthful.

Where to use them: Anytime you want to make an impression of being efficient, cool and modern with a little bit of an adventurous flair.

Personality Type: A Capella, Fusion, Pop.

Examples: *Christian Dior Dune, Davidoff Cool Water Woman, Giorgio Beverly Hills Ocean Dream, L'eau de issy.*

Creating Your Own

If you don't fancy going by one of the standard categories, there are a few services available to help you create a custom-made scent just for you. Some of these are available for you to order online, for example www.createyourownfragrance.com, or if you fancy taking a day out to create one, then look up www.theperfumestudio.com who host group perfume classes for individuals. There are also a few boutique style organisations who will do a 1-to-1 perfume creation session for you. This is the option that I went for, to create a beautiful flori-ental fusion that works perfectly for me.

Although your perfume can be a type of signature, you don't have to wear it like a uniform. Just as you have different wardrobes for summer and winter, you can also have different perfumes for day and night, or for different times of year. See what feels good to you, and build up a small selection of different types of scent that you love.

Applying Perfume

The most common advice on applying perfume is to apply it to your pulse points of the wrist and throat. A tip from the french perfume houses is to also apply a drop behind each knee and in your cleavage (perhaps just for the ladies!) Remember do NOT over apply perfume. A little can go a long way, so please don't think that over-applying will make it last longer. Over applying can actually be a complete turn off, so subtlety is the order of the day.

Reapplying the perfume throughout the day is also not recommended. After a while, your own nose will become desensitized to the scent, but others will still be able to pick it up, and you don't want to get to the stage where you have overdone it.

Chapter Summary

- Scents are one of the most popular ways to trigger the subconscious mind, to help you send out the signals that you want to.
- Perfumes are a bouquet. They consist of base, middle and top notes, which evaporate at different stages.
- Perfumes are available in the following families:

Perfume Type	Personality Type	Mood
Green	A Capella, House	Energetic, Sporty, Vibrant
Fresh	A Capella, Easy Listening, House, Pop	Young, Funky, Vibrant
Floral	Ballad, Opera, Easy Listening, Jazz, Bossa Nova and Symphony	Romantic, Feminine, Caring
Oriental	Symphony, Bossa Nova, Jazz, Big Band and Fusion	Seductive, Powerful, Exotic
Woody	Soul, A Capella and Easy Listening	Strong, protective, explorer
Spicy	Fusion, Big Band, Jazz, Bossa Nova, Easy Listening	Nurturing, deep, happy
Oceanic	A Capella, Fusion, Pop	Efficient, Cool, Young

Apply perfume to your pulse points and throat, and remember not to overdo it!

PART 3

BEING CAPTIVATING: THE PRESENCE

"The only thing worse than being talked about is not being talked about"
Oscar Wilde

Chapter 11

"I couldn't possibly go on stage!"
Instant Ways to Boost Your Confidence

"Be who you're and say what you feel because those who mind don't matter and those who matter don't mind"
Dr. Seuss

What is it that truly makes someone completely alluring? Despite spending the last five chapters talking about how we look, funnily enough, it's not always the good-looking girls who get all the success and attention. In fact, ANYONE can have a captivating presence, as long as they know how to get 'it' and work 'it' to their advantage.

So what is 'it'? The 'it' that gets people noticed?

The 'it' is very simple – it's confidence. Without a shot of confidence, all the styling in the world will not get you the results that you're looking for, as people can smell nervousness a mile off!

On the other hand, when you're comfortable with yourself and who you are, it shines in absolutely everything that you do. One of the biggest secrets I tell my clients is this: *'nothing is more important than how you feel about yourself.'*

The first head-turner secret is that you don't *have* to be Marilyn. Of course, if you've been blessed with good looks, use them, but have you ever met someone who is not obviously good looking, yet you're *just drawn to them*? What is that special X factor and how do they work it? There's only one little secret that I need to let you in on.

In order to *be* a head turner, you have to *believe* you're a head turner.

If you start telling yourself this, or any other belief you want to take on for that matter, you'll eventually start to believe it to be true and this will automatically be reflected in your body language.

Don't think you're there yet? Listen up, with a little bit of effort *anyone* can exude that air of confidence.

Shay's Story

I used to be an incredibly shy teenager. Even ordering something in McDonalds was a big deal for me because I actually had to talk to another person! The idea of that interaction was enough to make me feel really self-conscious and shy. I never actually wanted to be that way, and over the years I learnt exactly how to make the shift. In my twenties, this lead to me becoming a qualified and practicing barrister, moonlighting as radio presenter, jazz vocalist and even as a stand up comedienne. All those careers involve making an impact and confidence is an absolute must, which friends and clients all believe I now exude.

So what changed? It's different for everyone, but I know for me, that I would always wish I were the warm, charismatic and engaging person everyone in the room wanted to talk to. The first step was, therefore, a desire to change the way I'd been acting. Without this desire, I would never have made the change. I then used each one of the following boosters as well as working through the processes I talk about in part one of this book, to get me to where I am today. The people I was most inspired by certainly weren't too shy to order a happy meal! I conjured up the worst possible scenario that could happen if I were to act like them, and then I balanced up the potential benefits. Of course, when I thought about it like that, there was nothing to lose and everything to gain from trying to exude a care-free and confident attitude, so I slowly let go of Shy Shay and started to act with confidence, so much so that when I got to law school, people actually started to describe me as 'fearless!'

The way you feel is going to affect everything about you; from the way you move, to the way you dress, to the way that you interact with others. The smallest shift in your attitude and the mental dialogue you have with yourself manifests in the image that you show to the world. If you believe you are a certain way, eventually people will start seeing you in that way. This goes for negative thoughts too. If you believe you're too shy or nervous to talk to that influential or attractive stranger, speak in public or step out of anything that's currently in your comfort zone, that's what others will see. Whatever it is you think about yourself, others will start to see in you too, so make sure from now on that you feel and think about more of those positive qualities. It can be as simple as saying something positive to yourself the first time you look in the mirror each morning and making this a habit for 30 days. Or perhaps writing, *"I am amazing at* [insert thing that you want to be amazing at]" on your toothbrush. It may all feel a little false at first, but if you try out saying positive things to yourself, even if it's in a small way, it'll eventually become a habit, and more importantly, you will start to *feel* it. If you're still having difficulties with this, I would strongly recommend that you spend a bit more time working through part one of this book to make you feel good, long term.

The best way to boost your confidence is to work on your inner self, the work we looked at in part one of this book. The more happy you are in yourself, the more respect you have for yourself, the more confident you will be, and the less you will worry about what everybody else might think of you. However, we all also have those short-term jitters when our nerves just take over, and I'm going to be sharing with you my favourite confidence boosters for you to use in those moments when you feel your knees knocking!

Dealing with Your Inner Critic

So what on earth is an 'inner critic?' Well, you know that really mean, nasty and unnecessarily horrible voice, image or feeling that goes through your mind? The one that tells you you're not good enough? That's your inner critic and we're going to work on banishing it for good! This *thing* is a *complete* a waste of your mental energy and time so you have everything to gain by learning how to get rid of it.

The starting point of turning off your inner critic is to establish how it sounds to you. Is she a mean voice in your head? Is she so loud that she drowns out your other thoughts? Or is she just someone that you see or feel now and again? Once you have decided who or what your inner critic is, let's play with switching it off!

The Volume Switch

Some of my clients have found it really useful to imagine that the critic is a person who has a volume button attached to them. If you can imagine your inner critic, you can definitely imagine them having a volume button! When they get *too* annoying, remember that you control both the critic, and its volume.

If you're about to go on stage, you can imagine that you have a physical button somewhere on your body, which switches the negative voices off when you touch it. The more you do this, the more effective it becomes, as the body will eventually become associated with this action. For my clients, I often recommend that this off button is either on their hand, so that it is a subtle action, or somewhere on their head so it is close to their mind, but you can of course choose anywhere that's comfortable to you as long as it's consistent.

The Power Song

If you need a sound to replace that of your inner critic, try and imagine your favourite song or piece of music drowning out its voice. Let this sound fill your head instead, so that you do not have to listen to what your inner critic is telling you. Do you remember John in *Ally McBeal*? He got his inspiration from Barry White. John was a shy character in the show, but when he wanted to chat up women, or in fact make any sort of move, he would play a Barry White song in his head in order to inspire him. Ridiculous? Far from it! This is a technique used by many of my successful clients and indeed people who perform on the world stage. The difference between them and John is that no one knows they are doing it. It works not only because the song they choose inspires a more confident mood, but also, they're drowning out the little voice inside that tells them they're not good enough. If your song is not on loud enough, remember to use the button to turn the volume up to its highest to make sure that voice is well and truly drowned out!

The Mantra

This is an adaptation of the music technique. If you're not particularly musical, or you want to go that step further and use something that *inspires you personally,* then you could try using a mantra, or a prayer if you're of a religious inclination. Some good examples of a mantra include:

> *'All I need is within me now.'* (Tony Robbins)
> *'Winners never quit and quitters never win.'* (Lisa Nichols)
> *'Universe Surprise and Delight me.'* (Sonia Choquette)

It is of course just as effective, sometimes even more so, to invent your own. The point of using this technique is to empower you and to drown out anything in your mind that is negative, so whichever way works best for you is the best way. Make sure that whichever incantation you use, that it is in the present tense, so that you feel that this is true of you *now* rather than imagining that it only applies to who you used to be or someone that you will become.

Changing Its Voice

If you're still struggling with your 'off' switch, you can try using this technique instead, or in conjunction with one of the others. Changing the voice, obviously still involves hearing the voice, but we are going to change it into something far less threatening, so that it does not bother you anymore. This step is particularly good if you're not musical or don't want to use the mantra. On the other hand, if you use all these techniques together, you'll gain even more power over your mind!

To start using this step, think about how the voice in your head sounds at the moment. What tone is it using? How deep is the voice? How loud is it? Now think of the voice as having a cartoon character's voice. Make it silly. Turn its volume down. Make it seductive. By making the voice less imposing or by changing it so that it sounds silly, you're less likely to take notice of it.

Maria's Story

Maria used to have quite a lot of negative self-talk going on in her mind. I asked her whose voice she was hearing when this negative chatter was happening and she said that it was her husband's, although she did not understand why, as he was very loving towards her. I asked her to imagine the same things being said, but having her husband say them to her in either a loving way, a seductive way or a Disney way. Disney was the ticket – it made her laugh and she immediately started taking those voices far less seriously.

Changing How It Looks and Feels

If you're the type of person that likes to picture things in your mind, or feel things by experiencing or touching them, you can also use any of the above techniques in a more visual or kinesthetic, touchy feely way, by imagining you can switch off the images or the feelings. If you're of a kinesthetic inclination, you'll definitely benefit from the relaxation techniques that I'll go through in the next chapter.

For those of you that want to play with the visuals, these are some ideas of what you can do:

Size: The bigger something is, the more scary it'll appear to you. A great place to start is to imagine your inner critic as being really small, or if it is a situation that bothers you, you can imagine the people involved being very small, to make them appear less intimidating.

Colour: Colour is also a very powerful stimulus. Things appear much scarier if they are in bold bright colours. You can also control this by making the colour of your inner critic black and white, or just extremely dull and faded.

Distance: The nearer things are, the more intimidating they appear. You can, therefore, imagine your inner critic being very distant from you, or the situation that you're fearful of, being very far away.

Taking Control: Here you can imagine just getting the better of your inner critic. For example, one of my clients loves the image of her inner critic being thrown in the rubbish bin as soon as it gets too annoying! You can use whatever works for you – even if you're not an aggressive person by nature!

Remember with all these techniques, that the person in charge of that little voice inside your head is you! You create every thought that runs through your mind. What runs through your mind is your choice, so if you have a negative little voice, remember, you rule it, and not the other way around. Given that you're in charge of it, allow yourself to turn it down. With a little bit of practice, you'll no longer have the need to listen to it dragging your confidence down. Use this in conjunction with some of the other techniques in this chapter in order to maximise the confidence that you feel!

Using Your Look to Boost Your Confidence

Having spent the last few chapters exploring the way you look, you'll be pleased to know that your image can also boost your ego too. I admit that I always feel better dressed in my favourite dress and red boots. For me, dressing well helps me carry myself better and face the big wide world with a huge shot of confidence. I am a great believer in dressing in a way that helps you to exude your true spirit. This means that the real you is supported in every way, and on some subconscious level, if you're dressed that way, you're much more likely to behave in a way that is consistent with it.

One client of mine, a lawyer who at playtime just exudes the spirit of sunshine, told me that she gained confidence through wearing red underwear under her grey or black work suits! That way, she would always wear something that represented her essence, even if no one else was aware of it at the time. For you, it could be that extra coat of lip-gloss or a splash of nice aftershave; anything that helps you to feel like a million dollars is a good thing in my book!

To me, this doesn't mean rushing down to the supermarket in your Diane Von Furstenburg dress, but do always remember to take pride in yourself. At the bottom of this is your own self-esteem, if you feel good in it – wear it! This, in turn, will help others to feel good about you too, and your energy will rub off on them.

Shifting Your Focus

Focus on Delighting the Audience

This method works whether you're facing a large audience or a 1-to-1 client. Whatever the situation, there's reason for you being there. On some level, you already have the skills and knowledge to deliver what is being asked of you in that moment, otherwise you would not be in that position. Usually, when we are feeling negative, we are focusing on ourselves, how *we* are going to be such a failure and how much the other person, or people, are going to dislike *us*. Shift your focus so that the question you're asking your mind is 'How can I best delight the audience?' or something along those lines. It is likely that you know your content, song or material inside out already, so as soon as you shift your focus to *them* rather than *you*, then you're much more likely to just rock the stage!

Change Your Surroundings

For this technique, you can simply imagine that you're in a location or in front of people that feel less threatening to you. For example, if you have practiced your speech in front of a friend or loved one you feel completely comfortable with, imagine that this is just another practice in front of them. If you, like me, practice your routines, songs and speeches in the car, pretend that this is just another practice in the car. If you prefer, you can also imagine a more high-pressure performance that you have done in the past and remind yourself that in comparison to that, this environment is a breeze! The important thing is that you imagine that the environment in front of you is much less threatening than you actually perceive it to be.

Having done stand up comedy, I didn't think anything would have set my heart racing faster than stepping out on stage! A close second, however, was my first performance as a Jazz Vocalist. I found out that there were around 120 people in the audience, and that I had been chosen to open the show. That was more than enough to give me my fair share of butterflies! I got on stage, still feeling quite nervous, but the techniques I used on the night were:

Changing the Venue
I imagined that I was singing in my car; a place which I love and where I feel completely comfortable. It allows me to sing without a fear of not being good enough.

Changing the People
The song I was singing was *Moondance*, which is fairly romantic. Even though I wasn't with anyone at the time, I imagined that I was singing the song to a fictitious person that I really loved.

Focusing on Delight
Many people had already told me that I had a great stage presence. I felt there might have been a reason *why* I was asked to open the show and it was, therefore, up to me to delight the audience than worry about myself.

These three techniques alone helped me to get through the song. It just goes to show that you don't have to use all the techniques to improve your performance, but a combination of them can work just fine. Use as many of them as you need to ensure that you're staying calm.

When all else fails, borrow someone else's confidence! Sometimes, the best thing to do is just to borrow someone else's confidence. Some of my clients have very successfully pretended that they are their favourite actors/actresses/comedians/singers and to embody some of their natural confidence. To use this technique, think about how your favourite actor would behave in the same situation by playing a role. By doing it often, you'll eventually feel that confidence grow and you'll start to make it your own.

Here's what you do. Think of a famous actor of actress who you admire for their confidence. Take a moment to pretend you're that person and act as you think they would in a social situation. Do you remember one of their coolest films where they exuded natural confidence and charm? What was it they did or said? How did they move? Copy their stance and it'll give you a confidence you never knew you had!

Penny's Story

Penny told me that she felt shy and ugly every time she went out. She was never short of appreciative glances from the opposite sex and even worked regularly as a model. In order to overcome her seemingly irrational fears, she thought about someone she saw as confident. The most confident person she could think of was Madonna. She thought about how Madonna would act in the same situations and whether she would feel shy or think of herself as ugly. Undoubtedly, Madonna would probably never let that kind of negative thinking stop her from getting exactly what she wanted. From then on, Penny imagined that she was Madonna when she went to parties. The more she started to pretend that she was confident, the more confident and attractive she started to appear to others and the more she began to believe that she could radiate that confidence convincingly without pretending.

Using the Actor Strategy with Your Higher Self

My personal favourite 'actor' to use is my own higher self. Some of you may be wondering what on earth a higher self is. To me, this is the best version of yourself, radiating all your best qualities and at some level, the 'you' that you really want to be. I like to think of mine as a representation of what God wanted me to be in this world. Although this may sound a little 'out there', there is really no better person to use, as this is really you at your best, so its worth a shot; even if you're feeling a bit skeptical right now.

If you're already persuaded, you may be wondering *who* your higher spirit actually is. The easiest way to find out is to get into a relaxed state, using one or a combination of the techniques described in the next chapter. Close your eyes and imagine yourself at your very best, the most radiant version of you and think about these questions:

> *When you strip away all the layers, negativity and the everyday life tarnish, who are you really at your core?*
> *What do you look like at your core?*
> *Which top three words come to your mind as a representation of who your spirit is?*
> *What is his or her name?*
> *How does he/she want to be portrayed in this world?*

Once you have had an opportunity to find your higher self, remember that you have a divine responsibility to always embody that spirit. Or if you don't believe in the divine, just try it anyway and do it for you because *nothing* is more attractive than you at your best. You're your higher self's vehicle for shining in this world, so give them an opportunity to be seen! Whenever you're in doubt, tune into your spirit again and ask him or her how they would most like to be portrayed through you. They will always have the answer.

Chapter Summary

- Take control of your mind and remember to turn off that internal power switch or drown it out with music, mantras or any other sound that makes you feel relaxed.
- Change the voice in your head so that it sounds funny, seductive, Disney or anything that is less threatening to you.
- Shift your focus from wondering what everybody thinks about you, to focusing on what would delight the people in front of you.
- Embody the spirit of your favourite actor or your higher self and borrow their confidence for the day.
- Imagine that you're in front of a different person or in a different venue that makes you feel more comfortable.

Chapter 12

Relaxation Techniques

"Fear is excitement without the breath"
Fritz Perls (as quoted by Gay Hendricks' *The Big Leap*)

It's the performer's nightmare. You know you're good. You know that you can blow them away with your knowledge, content and experience. But then your dreaded nerves kick in. The great news is, the more that you perform, the less those nerves get over time, although its likely that you'll still get some residual butterflies at times, (we all do!) the secret is being able to manage those butterflies in a way that makes them work for you! I'm going to give you the *best* technique to get over the butterflies, which is to *breathe!*

I know this doesn't immediately sound like a magical solution, especially when you're suffering from nerves. However, breathing helps your physiology by adding oxygen to your system, which has an automatic calming affect on your nervous system. Our physiological state has the *greatest* effect on our emotional state, therefore, managing one, will automatically help you to cure the other. In relation to breath specifically, you will see from the quote at the beginning of this chapter that the only difference between fear and excitement is breath. Both emotions produce a similar chemical reaction in our body, perhaps it's the reason why a scary roller coaster is also very thrilling. So next time you feel fear, I would highly encourage you to take a long breath, as if you were having a nourishing meal and allow yourself to instantly notice the difference in your body.

Use the rest of this chapter as a reference guide when you feel it is appropriate. A lot of the techniques will be appropriate for you to use just before a stressful event, such as going on stage, or meeting an important client, but if you integrate breathing exercises into your everyday life, you will benefit from additional positive affects to your health, such as a healthy blood pressure, improved concentration and even reducing muscle tension!

Quick Techniques for Relaxation

Plus Minus Technique

This is the first breathing technique I ever started using on myself. The best way to use this technique is to sit comfortably and close your eyes, but if you're literally just about to go on stage, you can of course do it while standing. Take deep breaths in through the nose and out through the mouth. With each of the breaths you take in, imagine that you're filling your stomach. With each breath you exhale, imagine that your stomach is being emptied of that air. Once you settle into a regular breathing pattern, you can start imagining that you are breathing in plus signs, or anything that makes you feel positive. These days, I tend to use white light, but you can use whatever works for you. On each out breath that you take, imagine that you're breathing out negative signs or whatever it is that makes you feel the most negative. My most frequent image is that of black smoke. After doing this for a few minutes, your mind will feel much more relaxed.

Focusing on One Object or Place

Once you have used the plus minus technique, or any other of the breathing techniques, you can then focus on an object or image in your mind that makes you feel at peace. The image can be as simple as that of a candle flame that you visualise, that you have to place your intense concentration on. Watch the flame flicker in your mind. Notice its colours or feel its warmth. Our mind doesn't often know the difference between conscious and subconscious experiences, so a few minutes of looking into a relaxing object, even if it is just in your mind, will work wonders.

If you do not like the idea of using a candle, you can also think of a place that makes you feel at peace. It could be the place where you see your higher self if you often visualise him or her, or it could simply be a place that you've once visited and that you have really loved. For me, it's Beachcomber Island beach in Fiji, at sunset, when all the partygoers stop and are fascinated by the beauty and perfection of the environment around them. At that moment in my life, I remember being absolutely transfixed by nature and it is a place that makes me relax. Think about what this place is for you, whether it's real or imagined, and go there in your mind every time you start feeling a little nervous!

Abdominal Breathing Technique

This technique is particularly useful for singers or speakers who are going to be using their voice over a sustained period of time.

Singers even use this technique when they are actually singing in order to hold sustained notes! We can all learn from this technique though as it is a very simple one to practice everyday to improve your circulation, stress levels and health in general. It is important to remember that when we take deep breaths, we make them deeper not by inhaling more air, but by completely exhaling the air that we have taken in.

To start using this technique, breathe in to the count of 5, but exhale to the count of 6. You can, of course, use any numbers that work for you, as long as the number of seconds you exhale for is longer than the number of seconds you inhale for. You can gently contract your abdominal muscles to allow the air to exhale. In order to assist you, you can place one hand on your chest and the other on your abdomen to make sure that your abdomen is rising higher than your chest, but this is not necessary once you get used to the technique. The idea behind this is to ensure that the air is going right to the base of your lungs.

The Sounds

This technique is a variation on the abdominal breath. To use this technique effectively, simply breathe in the same way as you would for the abdominal breathing technique, but each time you breathe out, you're going to be making a sound. The first way that you can do this is by using a humming sound. If you go with this technique, make the humming sound for as long as possible, pulling your stomach in as you're doing it, so that you can squeeze out as much sound as possible. You then relax. The feeling of contracting, then relaxing, as with the progressive muscle relaxation technique, will deepen the level of relaxation you can feel.

Another variation using sound energy with your breathing is to breath out to the sound of 'ah'. This provides an extra release of tension in your body by engaging your vocal chords to release the tension as well as your breath.

Alternative Nostril Breathing

This is a technique borrowed from the world of yoga. It operates to bring the two hemispheres of your brain into harmony, so that your mind and body will feel totally relaxed. All you're going to do here is to breathe in through one side of your nostrils and breathe out through the other side of your nostrils. Breathe IN through your RIGHT nostril and OUT through your LEFT. Then back IN through the LEFT and OUT through your RIGHT. Use one finger to block the side of the nostril that you're not using. Repeat this process for 2 minutes, or for as long as you feel comfortable. You will notice a stark difference after only a few minutes. This one is especially useful before you go on stage, or before you're about to encounter a situation in which you're likely to feel nervous.

Relaxation Techniques to Use at Home

Progressive Muscle Relaxation
This technique can take a little more time, and for this reason it is probably best as a general relaxation technique rather than the

main one for you to use before you go on stage. I tend to use this one on the nights that I can't sleep – I don't think I have ever finished the whole exercise without drifting off! So this one will *definitely* relax you. Perhaps a bit *too* much, so be comfy before you start...

Here's what you do. Think of each part of your body individually, starting from your head all the way down to your toes, or from your toes all the way up to your head, and one at a time, contract and relax each muscle. You can also just let your awareness shift to the muscles, one at a time, and pay attention to each muscle for 30-40 seconds. Obviously you don't have to have a stopwatch – a guesstimate is fine. If you're using the contract/relax technique, contract your muscles for about 5 seconds, then relax for 30, until you've paid attention to each and every muscle in your body. If you do this one on a regular basis, it is likely to bring a far greater degree of calmness to your energy. This can also have an amazing affect on your clients and audiences, as it will make them feel much safer and calmer in your company.

The Breath of Life

The 'Breath of Life' is a technique taught by Sonia Choquette, who states that she uses this technique every morning prior to doing her own intuitive work. This technique is the one that not only energises her, but puts her own vibration at its highest. This really makes her feel at her intuitive best. Having tried this technique myself, I wholeheartedly recommended it for those of you that have the space to do it.

It involves putting on a piece of music that feels fast, yet high vibrational to you for approximately too minutes. As you listen to the music, you dance around your room, shaking off any tension with your arms and legs to the sound of "ha!" This is a development on the 'sound' breathing techniques; as well as using your voice; here you're also engaging your body to release any tension that you may feel. This is an excellent technique to use, even if you feel a little silly doing it – no one needs to know your secret after all! It can also be difficult to keep going for the full 2 minutes, but keep at it. When the song is finished, you truly will feel fantastic!

Other Energising Breathing Techniques

The Bellows Technique (The Stimulating Breath)

This technique is a gift if you're feeling a lull in your energy levels. It is particularly good if you have been driving for hours to get to a gig or client, and want to make sure that you're on form before you go in and meet them, although of course you probably don't want to start doing this in front of them! And it's much healthier than going for a quick shot of caffeine.

To start using this technique, stand up straight and comfortably, and breathe in and out of your nose as fast a possible. Both breaths should be equal in length, with as many as 2-3 inhales and exhales per second. It is the same sort of speed that you would use to pump air into something, except here you're pumping air into yourself to give you more vitality. This only needs to be done for about 15 seconds. Definitely don't overdo it, as you may start to feel a little faint, but as long as you can do this in moderation, this is an excellent technique for a quick 'pick me up.' If you want to enhance the sensation of this breath, you can also add arm movements, and pretend that you're playing an invisible accordion, as if you were pumping yourself up with air. This will add to the energy that you will already feel by using this technique.

Circular Breathing

This is a variation on the bellows technique, which is one to use if the bellows make you feel a bit too lightheaded. In this variation, you will pretend that your nose and mouth work as a circle, so that there is no gap between your in breath and your out breath. It is sometimes called the continuous breath for this reason. It won't make you as energised as the bellows technique, but it will calm your mind down significantly as you will be concentrating on making your breath a 'circle' rather than letting other thoughts wonder into your mind.

Other Relaxation Techniques

There are many other techniques that will relax you that don't involve having to work with your breath. One of the best examples I have encountered is the Emotional Freedom Technique. (Otherwise known as tapping.) It is a very popular technique, used not only for stress, but also for emotional or physical pain, unhelpful cravings, and in summary any emotion that you want to get rid of. It is based on the fact that we have different meridian points in our bodies. When we lightly 'tap' these points with our index finger and middle finger, the energy stored in these meridian points, in relation to your pain or stress, is released so that the impact of that emotion on you reduces vastly and in many cases even stops.

The meridian points in the body are shown in the illustration opposite.

Before you start tapping each of the meridian points in turn, think about the emotion that you're feeling. What is the emotion? If the emotion were to have a colour, what colour would it be? If the emotion were to have a shape, what shape would it take on? What are the words that you would use to describe the emotion? And lastly, on a scale of 0 – 10, 10 being completely unbearable, and 0 being that it does not disturb you at all, how would you rate the emotion or pain?

Now that you have the answer to these questions, start progressively tapping each of the meridian points in your body in the sequence that is shown. As you tap, say the words *'even*

though I feel this (pain/emotion), this (colour), this (shape), I completely love and accept myself.' Slowly progress through all the meridian points. As you tap the meridian points, state the colour, emotion, shape or any other words that come to you that are relevant to the situation. You should notice that the number that you picked at the start of the exercise to rate the emotion will have gone down.

Shay's Story

I first tried this technique when I was lying awake with excruciating wisdom tooth pain. I was about to go downstairs to reach for my parac-etamol bottle, but in a stroke of inspiration, I decided to try EFT instead, having learnt this technique a few weeks earlier. I couldn't believe that it actually worked to lessen the pain that I felt, allowing me to have a good night's sleep. I have used the technique ever since, any time I felt nervous or in pain and with clients, anytime I have felt that they could do with the help.

Another great technique that you can learn more about is the Alexander Technique, which focuses on working with your posture to not only help with your confidence, but also for your general health. One technique I still remind myself to use, both standing and walking, is to think of a piece of string, attached to the top of your head gently pulling upwards. This not only makes sure that you posture is upright, but walking with a confident posture such as this one will work wonders in improving your state of mind. If you're drawn to the Alexander Technique, I would greatly encourage a few sessions with a specialist practitioner, as regular sessions can work wonders on your performance, without you even realising why.

Chapter Summary

Breathing is one of the best techniques for relaxation. The techniques can be used either just before you go on stage, or on a regular basis for general well-being.

1. There are many different types of breathing techniques. The ones discussed in this chapter are:
   (a) Plus Minus Technique
   (b) Visualising a calming object or place
   (c) Progressive Muscle Relaxation
   (d) Abdominal Breathing
   (e) The Bellows
   (f) Circular Breathing
   (g) The Sounds
   (h) The Breath of Life
   (i) Alternative Nostril Breathing

2. Other techniques for relaxation include EFT and the Alexander technique, for which I would highly

recommend a few sessions with a practitioner if you are drawn to using these techniques on a more long term basis.

Chapter 13

"No one takes me seriously"
Oozing Authority with Your Voice

"The Human Voice is the organ of the Soul"
Henry Wadsworth Longfellow

For some, having an amazing voice is one of the biggest attraction factors. For many, a lovely voice is just an added bonus, although of course what is considered as lovely is *highly* subjective. Of course we aren't all blessed with the dulcet tones of Barry White or Ella Fitzgerald. Fortunately, this isn't necessary to increase your connection with someone, and of course, the more connection you establish with someone, the more authority you will ooze in relation to them. In relation to your voice in general, most people are only looking for two things; that your voice is in keeping with your look, body language, and message and that it connects to them in some way.

Margaret Thatcher's Story

Margaret Thatcher, despite being one of the most well-known British Prime Ministers of our time, was not born into a privileged background. Her beginnings were modest, yet she was fiercely ambitious. When Margaret Thatcher decided to enter politics, she was aware that her image, body language and voice needed to match the public's expectation of her. She was clearly very intelligent, but moulding her image, body language and voice into something that would be expected of her, for the position that she wanted, was vital in order for people to take her seriously. Amongst other specialist help, she famously took elocution lessons in order to evoke the gravitas and respect that she eventually did.

I would almost always, of course, recommend that you are yourself. However, my advice is that you go a step further, and as with every other aspect of your personal presence, you need to ensure that what you reflect is 'you' at your best. I.e. that you're the embodiment of your higher self. Margaret Thatcher clearly felt that her true self had not been allowed to develop over the years, so she embarked on a journey of undertaking a lot of work on herself in order to embody the person that she felt she was truly meant to be. She ended up moulding herself to fit a role that she wanted. For the rest of us, I would encourage that you consider where you want to be and tailor all aspects of your presence to suit that role; including your voice.

A good place to start in relation to your own voice, is to assess where you are at the moment and really think about the sound that it makes. What impression do you want to make with your voice? A great starting point to assess yourself is to record yourself speaking, using different tonalities and inflections in your voice. What sounds the most pleasing to you? A voice is made up of many different aspects. These are just a few for you to think about as you listen back to yourself.

Pitch

Is your voice high or low? As a general rule, lower pitched voices are more soothing to hear and can also carry better. You can develop a better pitch in your voice by staying relaxed and practicing humming to yourself.

Inflections

Addicting inflection to your voice is like having different notes in a piece of music. You wouldn't want to listen to a song with just one note in the whole song would you? If you did, this could get quite boring after a while. No inflection leads to monotony, and you may end up with people nodding off in the audience! Also be careful where your inflections actually are. For example, if you end sentences with an upward tone, this can make you sound doubtful, or can imply that you're asking a question. If you end them with a downward tone, this can make you sound far more authoritative. Adding as much colour as you can to your speech makes you far more exciting to listen to, and makes you appear relaxed and confident.

Rhythm and Pacing

This refers to the speed of your speech. For example, if you're doing an inspirational talk, with any sort of closed eye exercises in the middle, clearly your pacing will vary rather a lot, depending on the style. Remember to get the balance right; speaking too quickly will mean the audience will feel lost, and speaking too slowly consistently will mean you just lose their interest. Public speaking pace is only slightly slower than conversational speech. Remember to also keep it varied; just as interval training at the gym burns your calories quicker (by keeping your body guessing), varying your pace will keep your audience engaged and curious about where you're going next.

Timbre

Timbre refers to the quality, richness and pleasantness of your voice. Certain voices are excellent at gaining an emotional connection with the audience. The best way to judge your timbre is to record your voice and experiment with what you or your friends think sounds best. Of course, we aren't all blessed with the vocal tones of Barry White (as a woman, you won't want to be anyway), but we CAN do the best with what we already have in order to deepen the emotional connection that an audience will feel with us.

Volume and Energy

Being as loud as possible when you're in a public speaking situation isn't necessarily what it's all about. Sometimes, lowering your voice can be very effective as it can make people lean in a little closer to you, although of course people need to be able to hear you too. You can appear just as energetic being softly spoken. The most important thing is to remember that your talk must be enthused with energy and excitement in some way. Nothing is more off putting than your audience being under the impression that you're just not interested in what you're taking about, or straining to hear you.

Articulation

The best voices speak very clearly. In order to really ensure clarity in your speech, practicing and mastering tongue twisters will really help you speak clearly so that everyone can understand you. Say each one a few times, and then speed them up, without blurring your words. Some examples of tongue twisters that you can try are:

> *She sells sea shells on the sea shore. The shells that she sells are sea shells I'm sure.*
> *If you notice this notice you will notice that this notice is not worth noticing.*
> *Red Lorry Yellow Lorry*
> *A box of biscuits, a box of mixed biscuits*
> *Eleven benevolent elephants*
> *Sunshine City*
> *She said she should sit*
> *Greek Grapes*
> *Mallory's Hourly Salary*

Pauses

Sometimes, one of the most powerful things you can do is to leave a moment of silence. Rather than being 'weak', pauses can allow your audience to think as they add emphasis and impact, and they are certainly more powerful than using fillers such as *um, er* or *like*. The odd few fillers are fine – you don't want to sound completely unnatural – but peppering your speech with them can sound unprofessional and annoying.

Phew. A lot to remember I know! One of the best ways to put this into practice is to just record yourself and listen to it back. Look at all the aspects that I have talked about in this chapter, and analyse your own voice. If you need some help, of course don't be afraid to get the opinions of your friends and family.

Shay's Story

I was a very shy young girl. Part of this shyness also translated into really cringing when I heard myself speak on a recording. I literally didn't want to do it. Yet I used to love the world of radio, and in my teenage years was working for a major London radio station, answering their calls. It eventually dawned on me that in order to ever do any more radio, I needed to get comfortable with listening to myself. I got comfortable by initially just forcing myself to listen back to my shows, and also by being brave and telling friends to tune in. I used all the techniques I talked about in chapter 1, together with just noticing the compliments that people paid me, without deflecting them. Eventually, I got to the stage where it became more comfortable. As soon as I found that comfort within myself, not only did I win a UK National broad-casting award as best female presenter, but I also became a Jazz vocalist. So I would encourage you to embrace your fear, listen back to yourself regardless and you never know where it could lead!

Don't forget to use all these tips and techniques in conjunction with the previous chapters in order to maximise your magnetism; the more you use them all together, the more capti-vating you will become.

Now that we've talked about preparing your voice, let's explore how to really intensify that connection when you're speaking to someone. This technique is based on the principle that people like people who are like them. You may be in the position of their guru or mentor, but on some level, the people that you speak to will want to feel that they relate to you in some way – even if it's with their subconscious rather than their conscious mind. For example, imagine a sales man talking very quickly and loudly. How well would they get on with a yoga teacher who spoke in a slow, calm and relaxed way? Chances are, they would probably irritate each other as the former would be frustrated by the slow pace and the latter would be feeling unaccustomed to such a pace-y energy! If you want to get on with the person, a great way to build an instant connection is see how you can *match* their tone, pace and pitch. You instantly increase the bond between you. Subconsciously, the other person will relate to you much quicker.

Matching the way someone talks doesn't just end there. Different people use different words or imagery to describe certain situations. A simple example of this would be someone who uses the work 'fabulous' a lot. If you notice they're using this as one of their main descriptive words, you can increase the subconscious bond between you by using the word 'fabulous' rather than another synonym.

On a more advanced level, by listening carefully to the way your potential lover talks, you can figure out whether they think in an auditory, kinesthetic, visual or intellectual way.

Visual

Visual people often think by picturing things in their minds. They'll use descriptive words and phrases such as 'I see' to indicate they've understood something. They're likely to describe things in great detail too. When it comes to learning new things, they prefer to see how something is done first in order to best absorb their new skill. About 60% of people think in a predominantly visual way, so there's a good chance that the person you're speaking to is a visual thinker. If you've picked up that your potential date is visual, your response should be visual too. You can do this by using some visual terminology or describing things by visualising them yourself in order to ensure you're communicating in a way that makes sense to them.

Auditory

Auditory people are more likely to use sound based words to describe things and they may be particularly attracted to auditory experiences such as live music. They learn by hearing or talking about things. About 30% of people think in an auditory way. If you've picked up that your potential date is auditory, try and use more auditory phrases such as 'I hear where you're coming from' or thinking about things with sounds as a reference to create a stronger bond with your date.

Kinesthetic

Kinesthetic people use the way they feel in order to express themselves. They're likely to respond particularly to touch and will use phrases such as 'I feel' when speaking. They're likely to learn by having a hands-on experience too, so they can feel how something is done, another great tip is how they shop! Internet shopping is definitely not for the kinesthetic – they'll want to pick their purchase up, to feel it and touch it, only then will they decide to buy. Only about 10% of people think in a predominantly kinesthetic way. If you've picked up that your potential date thinks in a kinesthetic way, try to match their language. The odd gentle, innocuous touch may not go amiss either as kinesthetic people are likely to be very tactile and respond well to touch.

Intellectual

Intellectual people will be driven by the way they think, they'll analyse situations rather than feel their way through a scenario. Small minorities of people think in a predominantly intellectual way, but there are some individuals out there who thrive on expressing themselves like this. Watch out for phrases such as '*I think*' and '*I believe that...*' Try using similar phrases if you suspect your potential date falls into this category.

Most of us use all of these methods of communicating, but rely on one in particular. Some people may use one form of expression or thought for certain topics over another. For example, you may think and express yourself in a kinesthetic way if you're thinking about your children, but an intellectual way if you're thinking about work. If you listen to your potential lover carefully, you'll start to pick up the types of language they use in certain scenarios. If you match this language, you'll create a better bond with them.

Lastly, it would be wrong to write a chapter about the use of voice, without also saying a few works about the importance of listening. Listening to what someone else has to say is just as important, if not more important, than what you are saying yourself. There are three different levels of listening -- passive, active and deep.

Passive

Passive listening is hearing. Imagine a woman having a conversation with a man while he's watching his favourite game on TV. He's probably not going to pay any attention to her at all. He will hear the sounds that she is making, but there won't be any understanding, let alone anything responsive! Clearly this is not the best form of listening when you're trying to engage with an audience or potential client!

Active

The second type of listening, active listening, is probably the most popular type of listening for most of us. Some ways to make active listening engaging are to ask more questions so that you can understand the subject matter under discussion better and to remember to maintain good eye contact and generally friendly body language such as smiling and nodding. Paraphrasing can also be useful in showing that you understand what a person is talking about. These signals will build someone's confidence in you and inspire him or her to talk more.

Deep

One of the rarest, yet most powerful forms of listening is deep listening. This means that you're truly engaged with the other person in body, mind and spirit. Every fibre of your being is paying attention to what they are saying to you, not only with their words but also with their eyes and their body language. Often, when you listen to the way something is said, and couple this with the person's movements and expressions, you'll find out everything you need to know about how they're feeling. So listen up and pay attention! The more you understand the person you're talking to, the more they'll warm to you.

Effective deep listening also means avoiding letting your desire to put your own points across be the dominant focus of the conversation. This is so powerful as it makes the other person feel very special and they'll respond amazingly to you. You're not in any way thinking ahead of the conversation or wondering how to respond; you're just listening and hanging on their every word. Now that's powerful! In fact, I did this with a business contact as recently as last week, and after about 5 minutes, she commented to me that she was astounded at how much she had felt comfortable with telling me, despite not knowing me that well as yet!

Of course, deep listening is not always going to be apprpriate for every circumstance. However, when you sense that it *is* appropriate, you can really give someone a gift by listening to them at a deep level. Some people may have literally never felt this sensation before. Listening to them on this level will also allow you to pick up on some of their words and phrases, or whether they are auditory, visual, kinesthetic or intellectual. If you match some of these words or phrases, or use terminology in a way that they would most relate to, this will subconsciously increase the bond between you, allowing you to be effortlessly captivating.

Chapter Summary

- Record your voice to analyse whether it is as captivating as you can make it. Use the following factors to determine what needs to change (if anything):
  Your Pitch and tone.
  The inflections that you have.
  Your rhythm and packing.
  Your Timbre.

The Volume and energy with which you speak.

How articulate you are. Remember, that you can improve this with the use of tongue twisters.

- Any pauses that you're making with your speech. Remember to remove any unnecessary fillers such as 'um' and 'like'.

- When you're speaking to someone else, remember that you can determine whether they are visual, auditory, kines-thetic or intellectual, just by listening to their words. If you match some of their key words or phrases, you can immediately strengthen the sub-conscious bond between you.

- There are three types of listening; passive, active and deep. Often, active listening will be the most appropriate type of listening to use, but there may be times when you can really give someone the gift of listening to them deeply and really getting a sense of who they are and how they feel.

Chapter 14

"Surely my content is more important than how I present it?"
Speaking Body Language

"We can do it!"

"I speak two languages, Body and English."
Mae West

So what happens if you've already courted attention with the way that you look, and the confidence that you're exuding? What do you actually *do* when you speak to someone or a group of people? Research shows that there is *nothing* more important than our body language. It makes up 55% of what other people take in when we speak. The other 45% is made up of our tonality and words; our words represent a mere 7%! So body languge really is one of the most important things for you to get right.

In order to change your body language, as with your voice, you must firstly be aware of where you are right now. Notice how you sit, how you stand, how you use you hands and legs, what you do while talking to someone. You can practice in front of a mirror, and if you're feeling *really* brave, film yourself and analyse what you're doing, before you try out your outstanding of body language techniques on the people around you. If you are just not brave enough to do the video camera bit, then it's your trusted friends and family to the rescue. What do they think of your body language? You'll want to find out if they think it's welcoming. For instance, if they didn't know you, would they come up and chat to you? What do they think you're thinking when you're stood at the bar? Friends and family can be very honest with you about how tense or relaxed you look. Subtle moves can make huge differences in how people perceive your personality or mood, so it's worth asking and finding out what yours say.

If you feel that you can improve some of the body language you're projecting, a great place to start is by watching people that you admire, and study and look at what sort of body languge they use. Use their most compelling movements and try and incorporate those into your own body language. If you already know what sort of body language you want to portray, you can visualise in your mind how you would sit, stand or move generally as the most open, confident, relaxed and friendly version of yourself. By visualising this in your mind first, you will make it much easier to emulate this in your physical reality. Even if this all feels a little fake at first, the more you do it, the more natural this will eventually become to you. New habits always take a little while to incorporate into your life, so adding a few little powerful pieces at a time can also work wonders.

One of the major keys to portraying the 'right' body language is to remember that it is completely influenced by your emotions. Your body language is completely influenced by your emotions and your emotions are completely influenced by your body language. If you start smiling a bit more you will feel happier, and if you naturally start thinking more happy thoughts, you will also start to smile more naturally. If you have worked through all the advice in part one of this book, you should already be in a good emotional state and your body language will automatically have improved in the process. Above all, it is important that your mind is relaxed and positive in situations where you want to impress. If you have improved your body language over time, you will find that your emotions will soon follow suit. As the link is so strong between the two, it is vital that make your emotional state as strong as possible, so that you have an automatic head start when it comes to your body language.

A great place to start if you want to physically see the link between your emotions and your body language is to try this exercise either alone or with a friend. You can even film yourself as you go through this exercise, so that you can get a real sense of what your body is doing as you feel the emotions that I have asked you to connect with.

Start by thinking about your *biggest* desire. Think about how much you want this desire. Now tell yourself that you're being ridiculous and that it will never happen. Feel the thought of this desire never being fulfilled. I know that this is a thought that completely depresses you. While you're in the state, think about the following questions:

How are you standing?
How are you looking at people (if there are people around you)?
What are your shoulders doing?

What are you doing with your arms?
How would you be walking?
How does this stance make you feel?

Now give your body a shake and release that emotion. You're going to change your vision. Think about that desire again. Think about how much you want it. Now feel the feeling of being *absolutely positively certain* that this desire will be fulfilled. Great place to be isn't it? As you're connecting with those feelings, think about the following questions:

How are you standing now?
What are your shoulders doing now?
What are you doing with your arms?
How would you be walking?
Where are you looking?
How does this stance make you feel in comparison?

For extra brownie points, you can go on to do the exercise by just feeling hope in your body rather than absolute positivity. Feel how *maybe* feels. It's a less attractive feeling isn't it?

Once you have been through these emotional states and observed your body language, think about which body language would be the most attractive for people to look at. Negative thoughts will automatically lead to a negative body stance, and the more positive your body language, the more attractive and magnetic you will become. If you're finding it difficult to think more positively initially, emulate the stance you took when you were imagining the feeling of having your ambition fulfilled. Try and adopt that stance. Smile. Look ahead or look up. When adopting positive body language, it's very difficult to sink back into your negative thought pattern.

Once you're confident that the body language you're portraying is positive, test yourself. If you haven't done so already, it is immensely effective to film yourself, particularly in a social situation if you're feeling very brave and watch it back afterwards. It'll show you the body language you display and, more importantly, you'll see yourself from other people's perspectives. If you're worried about the body language you're using or have had negative feedback from anyone, this is the perfect exercise for you.

Martin's Story

One of my clients, Martin, found it very difficult to relax in social situations. As part of a coaching exercise, I decided to take him to a 40s themed party; he really wanted to get to the stage where he enjoyed being at a party like that.

The fact that he felt uncomfortable showed in his body language instantly. He looked very uptight and nervous. In his shyer moments, his shoulders were hunched too far forward and in his braver moments, they were too far back. His expression changed between one of extreme discomfort and one of sheer determination, rather than his body language telling people that he was simply enjoying the environment.

His body language was so negative that everyone he tried to talk to would appear to back off as soon as they could. It was painful to watch, but taught him a very valuable lesson. Martin had agreed to be videoed that evening and it was only when he saw the footage, did he understand how others saw him... it was this that changed his future!

Now let's look at some specific body language techniques. In my opinion, one of the easiest places to start is with your eyes. The eyes have often been described as the windows to our soul and can say so much. If you're speaking to anyone that is particularly perceptive, any discomfort can immediately be given away with your eyes if you're not careful. On the plus side, your eyes are enough to irradiate a warmth or sincerity, sometimes even enough to cross a language barrier!

Shay's Story

I was in Court on one occasion, representing a teenage girl who had been arrested and put in jail. Although the offence was not a serious one, the police had put her in jail as she did not speak any English and was unable to give the police a fixed home address. They, therefore, needed to put her in jail to ensure her attendance at Court. When I first met her, she was clearly very frightened of the situation, and although I could not speak her language, I know that she sensed that I was going to look after her to the best of my ability when in Court, just through the warmth that I consciously tried to show her, primarily through my eyes. When our interpreter arrived at Court later that day, they shared with me that she had been truly appreciative of the treatment that she had received from me, and it just went to show me how powerful body language could be.

So what does it take to have good eye contact? A great place to start is to imagine that you're smiling inwardly. If you do this, your eyes will automatically have a smile in them. If you're in a room where you want to make new connections, try thinking to yourself 'I know there are some amazing people here to get to know'. If you want to exude a bit more of a cheeky nature, you can even start thinking naughty thoughts in your mind, to give your eyes a bit of a fun and mischievous glint. This can work especially well if you're speaking to the opposite sex, even if you're not interested in them in *that* way!

The next thing to remember is that you have the ability to make someone feel really special by simply maintaining, and holding, eye contact with them. You'll be seen as very attentive, warm and understanding and it will probably lead to a deeper conversation as a result. When my clients use eye contact more, people open up to them more. What you're doing is making someone feel like the only person in the room and that nothing is more important than they are right at that moment. Combine it with the deep listening technique in the last chapter, and you can really weave some captivating magic!

Maintaining strong eye contact is essential when it comes to impressing. There is nothing more off putting than if you keep looking at your watch, or the next person in the room to talk to, or gazing down at your phone to text while conversing. If you do this, you'll just come across as disinterested, bored and rude! Contrast this to someone who is almost unable to take his or her eyes off you? Of course don't get creepy and stare at someone all evening or inspect their face as if they were under a microscope! Just maintain eye contact for slightly longer than you should to hold their attention and make them feel like they're the only person you're interested in talking to at that very moment – completely magnetic! If you're a little shy about eye contact, I would highly recommend that you learn from my childhood story below, and try out some dance lessons...

Shay's Story

I remember being very shy when I was in my teens. Being that way inclined, I don't even know what possessed me to start ballroom dancing. Obviously in that setting, you're in very close proximity to someone of the opposite sex. Having someone look at me for a prolonged period of time not only made me incredibly nervous, I actually just wanted to run and hide. Then I shifted my thinking and thought 'honestly, what's the worst that could happen?' After a mere few lessons, the sensation started to not bother me at all. These days, the way that I look at people has been described as anything from 'flirtatious' to 'magnetic', and it's simply because I am not afraid to not only look at someone, but look at exactly what their eyes are telling me, making people aware that I am genuinely interested in them.

My second favourite body language technique is just as simple. Smile.

If you see someone in the room that you really want to speak to, there is a no more effective way to start a conversation than to smile at them first. That way, they know that they are going to get a friendly reception as soon as a conversation between you takes place. Besides, happy people are particularly magnetic and a joy to be around! Imagine how much someone could make *your* day just by flashing you a warm smile meant just for you, even if you're not attracted to him or her? By smiling, you're giving a warm, positive boost to someone else and what better way to make someone feel good?

The best way to flash a sincere smile at someone is to catch someone's eye first. If you pause for a second, and then let a warm smile spread across your face, that person will know that your smile was meant just for them, rather than them thinking you're insincere, or that you just have a constant smile plastered on your face. Waiting that split second can escalate the sincerity that someone will feel from you.

If you're feeling too shy to smile at someone first, you can try visualising your ideal scenario first. Before you go out and start smiling at people at networking events, imagine yourself in that scenario first. Imagine a room full of your ideal clients and business contacts reacting very warmly towards you, just because you have taken the step of smiling at them first. You can even imagine in the scenario, that in flashing the smile, they have been immediately drawn to approach you rather than the other way around! The more you imagine yourself being able to do this, the more likely you are to be able to do it in real life. Your conscious and subconscious mind are so strongly linked that when you actually come to do this, you'll genuinely feel as though you've done it before and it really won't seem like such a big deal.

If you really want to get out of your comfort zone, you could even try the 'winking game'. I don't recommend that you try this in a business setting, but you can try it when you're out with friends one day just to boost your confidence. After all, if you have had a positive reaction when you have been out and winked at random strangers, how big a deal is a smile really? To play the winking game is simple. Remember, it doesn't matter if you're attracted to a person or not – all you need to do is to catch their eye and wink at them. The aim with this game is to build your own confidence and give the other person an ego boost. I've tried this together with friends and clients, in crowded places and safe settings. Every time we've done it, everyone we've winked at has responded with a smile or some sort of warm or appreciative gesture. We may have even made someone's day. Remember, this was an indiscriminate exercise. We winked at people whether or not we fancied them and every single person appeared to be flattered by the attention. The worst that could happen was that they could walk away, and in the long run how bad is that really?

Once you have a person speaking to you, one of the most powerful things that you can do to build rapport is to 'match' or 'mirror' their body language. We already talked about using certain words and phrases that the person you're conversing with uses in order to strengthen that subconscious bond between you in the last chapter, but using some of their body language can really intensify that connection.

For example, have you ever watched couples in restaurants or best friends talking to each other? One thing they're likely to have in common is that their mannerisms will be the same and they'll do the same things at the same time. For example, in a restaurant, a very connected couple may reach for their drinks at the same time without even realising. This is matching or mirroring; either they're doing exactly the same thing, or they're acting as each other's 'mirror' so they're moving in the same way. Most people don't even realise that matching or mirroring is happening; it's a subconscious link between two people who like each other. Obviously don't react instantly and don't copy *every* movement that the other person makes as you may just scare them. But a few mirroring movements, will have you connecting even more deeply on a subconscious level.

One of the reasons that our subconscious mind reacts so strongly to matching or mirroring movements is that if we emulate someone's body language, it gives us a very powerful insight into what that person is thinking. It stimulates a subconscious connection without the other person even knowing that you're doing it. If you go as far as matching someone's breathing, you'll probably go as far as feeling the *exact* feelings that they are feeling. If you want to try this as an experiment, pair up with someone and ask him or her to imagine a moment where they experienced a powerful emotion – something you don't know about. Ask them to replicate the exact body language and breathing patterns they were experiencing in that moment. You then have to copy *exactly* what the other person is doing. You can then almost guess, and in some cases even visualise, the moment the person was in.

Andrew's Story

I tried the exercise described above with Andrew. I suggested that we do this exercise and asked him to remember a powerful emotion by using his body language to tell me about it. He got into a strong standing position and started breathing, as he would have done then. Once he got into the correct position for the moment he was focusing on, I copied exactly what he did. I focused on what the position and breathing pattern was telling me. For a reason unknown to me at the time, I was imagining a clear blue sky in the middle of a field with lots of people standing around me looking happy and excited. I felt exhilarated and a real sense of pride, but I had no idea why.

When Andrew and I stopped mirroring each other, I asked him to describe the moment he'd been imagining. He told me that he'd visualised the moment he'd just won a shot-put competition. He'd been outdoors, in a sports ground on a beautiful day and there were many spectators around him. It was amazing to understand just how much I'd picked up about what he'd been feeling, just by copying his body language.

The example above is an extreme one. Clearly you can't go into networking events and copy people that you want to talk to, without them being worried about your state of mind or intentions! However, it is amazing just how much you *can* match or mirror someone without them consciously noticing. You want to do just enough to make them feel comfortable around you, so if you were to decide to smile or initiate a conversation, they'd feel happy to respond back to you.

If you match or mirror another person's body language you'll establish a subconscious bond between the pair of you before you even say a word! If they're standing upright at a bar, you could do the same. If they have one elbow leaning on the bar, you could do that. If they're sitting with their legs crossed, doing that will mirror their stance, making a connection between the two of you. You can even try and do things such as reaching for your drink at the same time they reach for theirs, like many couples or close friends do. By matching or mirroring someone, you're instantly and automatically becoming closer to them, as well as getting a real insight into how they feel.

Here are some of my other favourite thoughts on body language for you to implement:

Space

Generally, the better you know someone, the closer you're allowed to stand to him or her. Everyone has their own individual comfort zone, and I admit, I do sometimes playfully cross the line when I feel it's appropriate, to get someone out of their comfort zone! However, as a general guide, most people have a comfort zone of about 2 small steps away from them. Moving in closer can increase the intimacy between you, but it can also make the person you're talking to step away or fold their arms. Any movement of this nature is telling you that they want you to 'keep back' so do read the signs and respect them. Above all, you want to be careful not to break the subconscious bond that you're trying to form.

Also in relation to space, the amount of space that you actually take up is indicative of how confident you are. Confident people tend to take up more space as they are not 'hiding' themselves in a corner and are looking very comfortable with where they are.

Speed

The speed of your movements can also give away your level of confidence. Confident people tend to move a bit slower and are decisive with their movements. This goes for many things. Walking slower not only makes you seem calmer and more confident, it will also make you feel less stressed. If someone addresses you, don't snap you're neck in their direction, turn it a bit more slowly instead.

Moving Too Quickly

You might not realise that your body often mirrors your internal emotional world. If you're feeling a bit nervous about the first date, it could be reflected in your body language, such as making fast movements while talking or eating. This first date body language mistake tells her you're nervous and maybe even insecure. The impression you want to make is that you're calm, collected and confident. So become more aware of your body and try to slow down your movements.

Relax

The shoulders are one of the first signs to give you away if you're feeling tense. If you consciously try and relax your shoulders, coupled with one of the breathing techniques described in chapter 12, this can work wonders for how relaxed you will appear. Too drooped and you can appear completely lacking in confidence, too raised can appear like you're trying to hard. Keeping your head up at the same time is also very helpful – as interesting as the floor may be, staring at it, is not going to make you appear more confident. If in doubt, look in the mirror, video yourself or ask someone close to you for an opinion on what looks best.

Leaning

Leaning slightly towards a person can show that you're interested in what they are saying. Leaning back slightly if you're seated can also indicate confidence. However, do not overdo either of these poses. If you lean in too much, you will really start to invade someone's space and in contrast if you lean back too much you may appear distant or arrogant. Fundamentally, tell yourself that you're interested in what the person is saying, and let your body language follow.

Don't Fidget

Fidgeting with objects, or your hands, is one of the number one nervousness give away – don't do it! Put your hands behind your back if you must. Fidgeting can also display a complete lack of confidence or disinterest in the person or people that you're talking to. If you know that you have a tendency to fidget during presentations, see if you have a lectern available, or at least something that you can put your hands on to keep them still. Above all, if you focus on the moment in question and show genuine interest in the person or people that you're talking to, your tendency to fidget should lessen significantly.

Placing of Your Hands

The placing of your hands, particularly when you're speaking in public, is extremely important in conveying the amount of gravitas or excitement that you want to convey with your speech. You will notice that most excited looking sales people often have their hands in the air. This positioning of the hands automatically makes your voice sound a lot more excitable. Compare this to just leaving your hands down by your side. This, in contrast, will make your voice sound disinterested. The ideal positioning for your hands, if you want to convey an air of authority, is to have them at the level of your navel. If you watch most accomplished speakers, you will notice that this is where they place their hands. Remember, you don't actually want to cross your hands as this adds an unnecessary barrier between you and the person that you're speaking to. You do not want to come across as defensive if you're trying to build a connection with someone.

The Anchor

Lastly, I thought I would end this chapter with a subconscious technique. If ever you feel that your energy is scattered and that your body language is all over the place, imagine that your body is completely grounded and completely supported by the floor, or your chair, or wherever you are at the time. You can imagine either an anchor dropping down from your spine and attaching you to the core of the earth, or roots underneath your feet performing the same function. This state of grounded-ness will really help you to calm down your movements and exude author-itative and engaging body language!

Chapter Summary

- Body Language makes up about 55% of people's impression of us. It is, therefore, one of the most important things for you to get right.
- First and foremost, your body language is influenced by

your emotions.

- Positive emotions lead to confident body language and vice versa.
- Always try and emulate a state of absolute certainty and confidence in situations where it is vital for you to portray good body language.
- Remember to maintain good eye contact and a happy, smiling demeanor.
- You can match or mirror the person you're conversing with to intensify the subconscious bond between you.

Good Body Language	Bad Body Language
Strong, firm handshake	Limp handshake
Leaning forward	Looking down
Good Eye Contact	Drooped shoulders
Altering facial expressions to match your words	Invading someone's space
Relaxed posture	Staring
Nodding	Folded arms
smile	Clenched hands
Slow, deliberate movements	Fidgeting
Mirroring the person you're speaking to	Touching face

Chapter 15

"I just want to be admired, appreciated and adored"
The Art of Connection

"The world is so empty if one thinks only of mountains, rivers and cities; but to know someone who thinks and feels with us, and who, though distant, is close to us in spirit, this makes the earth for us an inhabited garden."
Johann Wolfgang Goeth

So, now that you've got tools and techniques to get over the scary part of actually being in front of your client, getting on the stage or simply being the best 'you' in life, let's take a moment to consolidate your favourite confidence boosting tips, make a list here, so that you have them to hand next time you need them!

....

....

....

....

....

....

Sales v Service

Let's now get into the actual business of speaking to people and ultimately getting on the stage, and being the best 'you' that you can possibly be. As you have learned throughout this book, what you *actually* say to someone is *never* as important as your body language when you're saying it. However, if you're an entrepreneur of any description, you have to not only get good at the art of sales, but also in my opinion, do it in a way that is elegant, rather than potentially coming across as sleazy. Nobody likes to be sold to, but everybody likes to buy, as long as the offer is right!

If you already have some experience of sales, you will be aware that you must always sell to either someone's pain or someone's pleasure. Human nature dictates that we will do much more to move away from pain than to move towards pleasure, but either approach can work. However, this theory won't actually serve you if you have made no effort to connect with the person you're selling to first.

The Dating Coach's Story

I attended one of T. Harv Eker's money seminars, where unsurprisingly a lot of entrepreneurs turned up wanting to learn how to make more money. In one of the breaks, a young woman approached a friend and I. Without saying a word to either of us, she handed us both her business card then ran off to hand out more to as many people as she could! The business card itself was not particularly impressive enough for me to want to do business with her, but more worryingly, her business was for an online dating service. My friend was clearly wearing her engagement and wedding rings and, therefore, would have had absolutely no desire to use the service. As for me, I had already worked as a dating coach, and although I was single at the time, had I wanted a dating coach, I would never dream of hiring someone for such a personal service who hadn't even spared the time to connect with me personally. The lady in question would have been far more successful if she had taken the time to nurture a connection with just one or two people in the audience, rather than wasting 50 business cards on people who had no attachment to her whatsoever.

Remember, nobody likes to be sold to, but everyone likes to buy. Ask yourself how you feel when people approach you with the hard sell when you have no interest in the product or no connection with the person. Not great is it? This is why I would like to encourage you, when you 'sell' to come from a place of really wanting to serve the person or people in front of you. If you're only doing something for the money, chances are, you're not living your life's passion or purpose anyway.

Assuming that you love doing what you do, and you want to share your gift with the world, focus on every 'sales conversation' being a 'service conversation.' Have faith in yourself that what you offer is of value, and remind yourself how much you want to serve the person in front of you. As soon as your business becomes about what you genuinely want to offer to the world, and is about what you can do to serve your clients, your energy becomes infectious and people are more likely to buy your products. The money you'll earn will then become a by-product of your primary aim of being of service, rather than your sole focus, and in turn people will want to buy more from you. Nobody will buy from someone who is just after their money.

The Internet Marketer's Story

I have met many Internet marketers in my time, but none quite so honest as this one. We sat next to each other at a Tony Robbins seminar and I asked him what drove him about doing Internet marketing. He answered that he thought it was a way to make money. I asked him if he had any other motivations to run this business. He told me that he didn't. Finally I asked him whether he was actually making any money from it. Unsurprisingly he was not. It was clear that he only had a financial motivation for making his business work, and as such he was finding it difficult to sell a product that he himself had absolutely no passion for.

Even if you do have passion for your product, you must still ensure that you don't come across as desperate for money. I understand that we may all have our bills to pay each month, but if you're feeling desperate, please go back to chapter 1 and work on your mindset. People can sense 'desperate energy' and if you come across in this way, you will still find business very challenging. If, however, you genuinely want to serve people and wholeheartedly believe in your own abundance, you're likely to do very well indeed.

Richard Branson's Story

Richard Branson started his career in his teens when he left school to run his own magazine. He does not try to sell Virgin products. He combined his utter faith in himself with his love of creativity to consistently take huge financial risks, but of course has always landed on his feet. His ethos behind creating the services that he does is to look at things he doesn't feel are being delivered at their best and make them better. In fact, he goes through life asking himself the question, 'How do I make this the best experience it can be?' It is not primarily about how much of a personal fortune he can amass for himself, although, after many years in that mindset, he has done so. From this place of service, you're in a state of mind where you genuinely want to share your gifts with the world rather than worrying about how many zeros can be added to your bank balance. Although the security of money is lovely, no one is going to want to do business with you if they sense that the only reason you're in business is to be rich.

If you're still wondering what to actually say to potential new clients, my best advice is to ask them as many questions as possible, so that you have a real insight into who they are and what they need. It's only when you can really tap into their psyche that you'll be able to find out exactly how to be of service to them. This is not about you showing off and not letting them get a word in edgeways. Be present. Listen to what they are telling you. The more that you can understand and connect with them, the more you're going to be able to serve them and the more they are going to be able to trust you.

In terms of the exact words to use, obviously there are many different people reading this book working in many different niches and industries. YOU are going to be the best expert on what *you* offer. But be aware that your sales offering will be a lot more effective if you focus on how they are going to benefit from your services rather than going on about how wonderful you are, which I know is always tempting! Lastly, for the more spiritually minded amongst you, remember to always remain open for God or whichever divine power you believe in, to utterly surprise and delight you. Stay present with the person you're talking to, and beyond that let your natural intuition lead the way. It may sound frustrating to advise you to just see what comes out, but if you're truly paying attention to the person with you, more often than not your natural intuition will not let you down.

How to Start a Conversation

If you're still wondering what to use as an 'opening', my favourite, in almost every circumstance, is the good old-fashioned smile! By smiling at someone, you're vastly improving the body language you project. It's impossible to smile a genuine smile and appear unfriendly at the same time. Someone with a warm smile and the personality to make you feel interesting, comfortable and generally wonderful will go much further than any clever or witty opener that you may have prepared. Of course, if you have your image just right, chances are that other people will be approaching you before you even have to worry about what to do next.

In a social setting, a good conversation opener if your smile is returned is a question or comment about the host and/or party or a compliment. There are four keys to giving the perfect compliment:

1. Keep them simple
2. Keep them respectful
3. Keep them sincere
4. Make them evidence-based

Evidence-based compliments ensure that what you're saying is not just empty praise. For example, *I think you're very successful* is a nice compliment, but nowhere near as powerful as; *'you deal with situations at work well because of how you think things through before you act. It makes you very successful.'*

If you think of a compliment, think about whether the person would actually appreciate it. Remember the person you like. How do they dress? How do they carry themselves? When you want to give a compliment, you'll be making a judgment call on how well your compliment will come across. By thinking of a specific situation to back up your compliment, you'll make it all the more powerful. So many people get compliments and never believe them. By putting evidence behind them, you're giving them a reason to believe you. It has a very different feel from simply telling someone they're successful just because you think it's your point of view. You're giving them an actual example of how you've observed them being successful. It shows you've thought the compliment through and shows you really mean what you say.

By following the four keys: simple, respect, sincerity and evidence-based, you won't embarrass the person you've complimented; you'll enhance their persona and they'll shine. Make sure you actually believe the compliments you're giving. Speak with sincerity and tell them why you think what you do. Evidence-based feedback is vital and will make the difference between someone brushing the compliment off and not taking you seriously, and feeling better than ever; even someone shy won't be able to resist your compliments if they're based in fact.

Avoid over complimenting. It has two effects; not only will you come across as needy and desperate, or worse still, fake. You'll also embarrass the person you're complimenting in the process.

Emma's Story

Emma was with Rich for two months. Initially she found him to be incredibly romantic and adored the attention. However, every time they spoke, Rich's main topic of conversation was how smart, beautiful and wonderful she was. He even went so far as to change his views about certain topics if Emma ever disagreed with him because 'Emma was so clever' and she must be right. After two months, she ended the relationship. What she really needed was a man that didn't hang on her every word.

Stick to a few well chosen evidence-based compliments as part of a wider, exciting conversation and you'll be building excellent foundations for a future.

During the Conversation

My favourite tip to keep a conversation going is to remember to make things easy for the other person. I always like to look into people's eyes to let them know that they have my full attention and to avoid little habits like looking at a watch, looking at my phone or staring out at other people in the crowd. Giving someone your undivided attention can make them feel very special indeed, but please use your discretion – you don't want to come across as sleazy or scarily fixated.

Another useful thing to think about is what would make things easy for the other person. What could you do to make someone feel comfortable talking to you? What would put *you* at ease if you were them? How do you most like to be spoken to? What makes you open up to people? Thinking about these questions will help you to make things as comfortable as possible for the person you want to speak to and will be your secret key in making sure that the people that you encounter not only have a positive impression of you, but completely adore you too! An awareness of what would make the other person feel comfortable and a genuine desire to put them at ease is all you need.

As discussed in the last chapter, about 80% of how you come across has nothing to do with what you say; it's primarily to do with your body language and the way that you say things.

When you're talking to someone new, it's likely that your mind is racing. What comes next? What do you say to a complete stranger? When 'attraction' is the only thing on your mind, how do you make sense of your thought processes?

The key to a successful conversation is to be attentive, to simply stop worrying as much. A simple 'hello' followed by conversation about the venue, your host (if you're at a party) or your immediate surroundings will start you off on neutral ground. If you're feeling brave, an evidence-based compliment can work too.

Having a few conversational topics up your sleeve is always a bonus. Keeping an eye on current events, listening to what your peers are talking about, and keeping a mental note of interesting things you've done, will all help you immensely.

Back to conversation though, and you'll be relieved to hear that you don't need to talk all the time. In fact, it's really important that you are listening, and are genuinely interested in what the other person is saying rather than focusing on telling people your life story. Listening is definitely a skill. Some people have an in-built understanding of how to listen, whilst others need to really work on their natural instincts to interrupt and finish people's sentences for them. Simply put, when you listen, you'll be asking more questions than telling your own stories. When you ask questions, the other person gets to talk more. They'll open up to you because you've asked a question in an open and inviting way. Open questions such as those starting with *who, what, when, where and how* work fantastically. It's almost impossible for someone to give you a one-word answer. *Why* questions can do the same thing if asked in the right tone.

If you find your mind going blank and have no idea what to say next, always take the topic back to the person you're talking to. It's true that most people's favourite topic of conversation is themselves; after all, it's a subject we ALL know about inside out. It also shows you're interested in finding out more about them too. If you couple this with incisive questions and good eye contact, people are much more likely to warm to you. Do make sure you're listening properly though. Whilst asking questions and seeming interested in them will score you some points, not remembering anything about them an hour later will take them all away again. On the other hand, if you remember little details they've been telling you and refer to them throughout the evening, you'll impress them no end.

When it comes to talking about yourself, avoid making it sound like you're self-obsessed. If the other person is asking lots of questions about you, try and return the questions and learn something about them too. Hand the spot light over to them too for an equal sharing of information.

The 'Loud Man' Story

I was in a restaurant recently watching two people having dinner. It was clear they were on a date and didn't know each other very well. The man was very loud and talkative and the lady was very demure. She wasn't contributing much to the conversation at all.

The way the man spoke overpowered the woman; he was showing off about people he'd met, what he'd done and was even laughing at his own jokes. And yes, he was talking so loud that I couldn't help but notice him from the next table.

Little did he know that his boisterous behaviour was going to end up in a book as a 'How not to' story! I'm quite sure that date wouldn't have led to a second one but what's worse is that I'm also sure he wouldn't have realised why. He came across as self-absorbed, arrogant and boring! This is your opportunity to avoid his behaviour.

Check you're not the 'Loud Man' (or woman) by making sure you're absolutely self-aware. Don't forget to watch for those body language signals that are always useful for giving you clues on whether topics are interesting and boring! Are they engaging with you? Are they laughing at your jokes and contributing something to the conversation themselves? Is their eye contact and body language looking positive and interested? If not, they're not! Shift your conversation and ask a few questions about them.

One of the best ways to keep a conversation going is to use humour and to keep things fun. Whilst you want the person to know something about you, it's vital to keep it light hearted. They won't want to know all about your darkest moments, business disasters or previous broken hearted love affairs!

On the Stage

So now that you've dealt with your fears and are able to connect with people one on one, how do you move this connection to the stage? Even on stage, this conversation or presentation is not about you. It's about the people in front of you. Your primary aim with them should be focusing on the question of how to absolutely delight them rather than focusing on how you're personally coming across. Beyond that, there are many different tools and techniques that you can use either individually or together to make sure that your stage presence is completely captivating!

Factors to Know in Advance

It's important that you know in advance:

- How much time you will have on stage
- Who your audience are
- Whether you will be required to take any questions

Once you have this information, you can prepare accordingly. Make sure that you research your topic appropriately so that you're in a position to take questions, even if the organiser has stated that you won't need to take questions. It's always best to know more content than you're going to present in your talk. You may always get people approach you at the end of the talk to ask you something, and you do not want to be perceived as anything less than the expert.

Writing Your Talk

If you're on stage for the purposes of giving a talk, chances are that you'll want to decide what you're going to say in advance. There are a few people who give talks from pure intuition, but these people are few and far between and it is not something that I would recommend that you do unless you already know that you're good at presenting in this way AND you've had feedback that you can.

One factor to remember is that people love stories. Even with the driest of topics, you can make the content far more compelling if you add personal stories to it. It will go some way to ensuring that you're captivating your audience by keeping their attention. For extra pizazz, throw in some humour; it is nearly always a good idea to make people laugh so that they feel instantly at ease in your presence.

Before the Big Day

Don't even dream of going on stage unless you *practice!* The better you know your material, the less likely you are to think that you're going to fall flat on your face once you get in front of the audience.

One of the best ways to prepare is to pretend that you know nothing about the topic and how you would like the topic to be explained to you from the viewpoint of a beginner. Of course, your audience may be very advanced and accomplished, so obviously the level needs to be pitched correctly. However, no one likes talks that go way over their head, so bear in mind that other people may not have as much specialist knowledge on your subject as you do. If you can also think of ways to keep the audience engaged by getting them to do activities and answering questions, this is great too – not only will you get a heightened interest in your talk, your audience will be learning a lot more from you by engaging more of their senses to learn your material.

Lastly, one of the most powerful things you can do is to visualise yourself doing brilliantly when you speak or perform. Imagine yourself on stage, full of confidence, with the audience hanging on your every word and being completely captivated by you! If this is a difficult leap for you to make, you can always go back to the techniques in chapters 3 and 6 for a helping hand. The more positively you can picture yourself, the better you're likely to do on the day!

On the Day

The big day is here! I would highly recommend starting the day with a short centering exercise such as a meditation, or if that isn't up your street, a few breathing techniques[1] just to make sure that you feel completely relaxed. Remember to give yourself plenty of time to get to the venue, so that you can be early and avoid any extra reasons for stress. If you arrive *really* early, you can even have some time to practice on the stage with your visual aids and microphone.

Another great reason for arriving early is to meet and greet the audience when they arrive. Not only can it give you a great insight into how to pitch your talk, but also it gives you a chance to get to know your audience so that you're speaking or performing in front of friends, not strangers. Remember that everyone in the room will want you to do well.

Just before you get on the stage, you may want to take a moment to loosen up and make sure that you feel as relaxed as possible. You can do this by:

Rolling your head around in circles, both ways, then looking from side to side.

Stretching.

Touching your toes, then very slowly standing up straight, moving only one muscle at a time.

Breathe!

You're On!

So this is the big moment! Whatever your topic, don't forget that you are there to entertain. You're also there to be as authentic as you can. Have you ever wondered how Ella Fitzgerald, or any other talented singer, has the power to move people with their presence? Well, they always give off the impression that they mean every word that they say and truly sing from the heart. Even if you're not a singer, remember that speaking or performing from your heart and soul, is far more authentic than simply reading things out and planning particular gestures to use on stage.

Not confident enough to let go of your notes? Well, although PowerPoint is great as a prompt, remember, whichever type of visual aid you use, it is an aid, and not your entire presentation. Although people are compelled to jot down the content from your slides, your talk should be just as engaging without them, so there is no need to put every word that you're intending to say on there. Your message will sound far more authentic if it comes from you, rather than your slides or cue cards. The same applies for singers, comedians and other types of performers; how awful does it look when you don't know your lyrics or material and you're having to read it off a music stand?! This can really interrupt the flow of what you're doing. If you really must have some cues, these are my favourites:

- Have your laptop on the stage with you with your PowerPoint notes on them, so that you can see them but no one else can. They are there for reference only though, so make sure you're not just reading them.
- If you're using a flip chart, you can try writing some keyword prompts in pencil at eye level to help you. If they are written in pencil, it is highly unlikely that the audience will see them, but you will have them there for security.
- If you can be really subtle about it, you can also write keywords on your hands. If you're someone that is likely to use a lot of open gestures, then bear in mind that this isn't going to look good, but could be perfect if you're singing at a microphone stand.
- If you're on a raised stage, you can have keyword prompts written in relatively big letters on a piece of paper on the floor. This works particularly well for singers struggling to remember lyrics; your keyword will simply be the first word of every line.

- If you find yourself needing a little extra thinking time, statements such as 'that's a really good question', or 'I'm glad you asked' will give you a little extra space, without the audience knowing that you're still thinking about the answer. If you really don't know, be honest, and suggest that you speak to the person afterwards about the issue that has been raised.

- As well as what you're saying, you must of course also be aware of your body language. Of course certain movements mean certain things, but planning them in a mechanical way can lose the authenticity that you should be bringing to the stage.

- Any movements that you use are an extension of your message, so they should not look false in any way. If you're in doubt, keep your hands at your navel, on the microphone or on a lectern; depending on what equipment you have at your disposal. A lot of people in the public speaking training world may advise you to keep your hands by your side. However, this can look like you're bored, nervous or unenthused about your message, so if you do choose to speak with your hands down by your side, make sure that you have an abundance of energy about you to compensate.

- One of the most important aspects of body language is the way that you use your eyes. One-on-one, it goes without saying that the person you're talking to (should you be interested in them in any way whatsoever!) should be engaging your full attention without you checking the time, checking out other people or any other distractions that are around you.

Addressing an Audience

In the case of an audience, it has often been said that you should focus on one part of the room and talk to this area. The area that you pick should be at the same eye level as the audience, or potentially a camera filming the event. I have certainly seen many speakers, and even well-known comedians, employ this strategy. My personal view is that this strategy displays their lack of connection with the audience in front of them, although of course, people watching on camera are unlikely to notice. If you have the confidence, it is far better to choose a few people, in different parts of the room to talk to, and give them as much of your warmth and vitality if you can. Remember, it isn't just about the decision makers and other important people in the room. Often they will seek opinions from their assistants and employees, so you don't want to make them feel less important. If all else fails, just remember that you're there to delight – and enjoy it! If you're not having this feeling, your eyes will be the first thing to give you away, so you'll need to change your focus quickly to ensure that you do feel this way.

Once you have your body language sorted out, remember to also pay attention to how you are using your voice. It goes without saying that you must make sure that you're projecting it so that the room can hear you. Imagine yourself speaking from your lungs or stomach rather than from your throat. This will give your voice more resonance in front of an audience. If you have arrived at the venue early and you have the luxury of a microphone, make sure that it works!

I would also recommend that you slow down. Not so much so that you sound dispassionate, but enough to let people absorb what you're actually saying. The added advantage in doing this is that speaking slower and giving yourself pauses, gives you a bit of extra thinking time. It also stops the sensation that your words come out before you've properly processed them in your head!

Shay's Story

Many years ago, when I was looking for my initial training as a

Barrister, I went to a few interviews with Chambers. At the time, I was already working on radio, and had not only got into the habit of talking quickly, but also being very conscious of not leaving 'dead air' time, so I'd fill any natural pauses too. Although I did get my first position quite easily, I remember one of my interviewers commenting that I should not be afraid to slow down my speed, and to pause at times. That comment has stayed with me ever since. 10 years later, I have had a number of comments from people about how they perceive me as speaking in an authoritative way; I would say that slowing my speech down has made a significant contribution to this.

If in doubt about any of these techniques, you can always watch how the great speakers and performers of our time do it. When I initially did my training as a barrister and comedienne, I spent countless hours watching other professionals in action. I was able to learn from their mistakes and observe things that they did that worked particularly well. I was also able to emulate what I thought were the best bits of their performance, before ever having to undertake either role. The other advantage of doing this is that you can always 'borrow' the confidence of a performer that you particularly admire. Emulate how they carry themselves. Think about what they would do in particular situations. Again, the gestures should not be pre-planned, but by borrowing their confidence, your body language is likely to be improved naturally.

Fiona's Story

Fiona is an agent for budding Jazz singers, wanting to find recording contracts and of course takes to the stage as a Jazz Vocalist herself. In her early career, she occasionally felt the nerves creep in during her performances. One night, we happened to be performing together. The organisers had me opening the show with 'Something's Gotta Give' and her following me with 'Misty'. I talked to her shortly before we went on stage to say that this was the exact sequence that Ella Fitzgerald had used for one of her televised concerts in the 60s. I said that I was sure her spirit was with us both that evening as we had been placed in that order, with those songs purely by chance. That was all we needed. Suddenly we became not just 'Fiona and Shay', but 'Fiona and Shay doing Ella' and it resulted in one of the best performances I have ever seen her do!

Even the best prep can leave you lost for words sometimes! When you feel like this, the best thing to do is to shift your focus. Remember to concentrate on your message rather than yourself as a simple shift in focus can honestly make the world of difference, and completely change the energy of your performance. Overall, believe that you will shine on stage, and you absolutely will!

Chapter Summary

- Focus on serving the person that is in front of you, not on how to sell to them.
- Sell to people's pain or pleasure by finding out a little about them first and seeing whether they may or may not be the ideal client for you.
- Ooze passion about what you do.
- A smile is always a great opener.
- If you use compliments, make them evidence-based.
- Maintain great eye contact, without being distracted by other things.
- Listen to what your customers and audience have to say. Their words are like gold dust to your business and it will allow you to find out exactly what you need to sell.
- Be prepared by researching, practicing, breathing and relaxing!
- Be aware of your body language on stage.
- If you're getting nervous, think about how the professionals do it and borrow their confidence for the day!

I hope that you have enjoyed this book. I always love to hear your stories and comments on how these techniques have helped you, or whether you have any of your own you would like to share, so email me at: **shay@shayallie.com.**

Of course if you would like any further assistance, I would be absolutely delighted to help you. There are a number of ways that you can continue your work with me:

The Blog

I regularly write articles or film short video clips on my blog available at **www.howtobecaptivating.com** to give you the latest advice on how to be captivating. Stay tuned, and I welcome your contributions for those of you that want to be involved in the Captivating Presence community.

The Books

The Grown Up Guide to Kiss Chase

If you want to learn to be captivating for the purpose of attracting the lover of your dreams, I have also written "The Grown Up Guide to Kiss Chase", which is especially for those of you that want to apply the Captivating Presence techniques to become magnetic to love.

Workshops

I regularly host workshops and speak at other events throughout the year. Please keep an eye on **www.howtobecaptivating.com** for forthcoming events.

Personal Consultations

My personal mission is to help as many people as I can, with the skills that I have, to ensure that they feel completely fulfilled in both their business and their life. I work with a small number of VIP clients each month, to ensure that all my clients receive individual attention. The clients I have worked with in the past have seen a significant shift in business and in their personal lives by applying these techniques in a way that is personalised to them. If you're interested in VIP mentoring, please contact me at: **shay@shayallie.com** leaving your phone number, and I will contact you to arrange a free introductory VIP consultation where we will identify the no.1 shift you need to make to ensure that your life and your business reaches the heights of success and happiness that you most desire. If we both feel it is appropriate, we will then decide on a mentoring package between us that best suits your needs.

Whatever way you choose to connect with me, I really look forward to learning more about you. In the meantime, I wish you success, happiness, love and complete fulfillment in your business and your life.

With all my love

Shay xoxo

**SASSY
BOOKS**

Hip, real and raw, SASSY books share authentic truths, spiritual insights and entrepreneurial witchcraft with women who want to kick ass in life and y'know...start revolutions.